LIGHT ME A CANDLE

LIGHT ME A CANDLE

Terry Dillon

Book Guild Publishing

Sussex, England

First published in Great Britain in 2011 by
The Book Guild Ltd
Pavilion View
19 New Road
Brighton, BN1 1UF

Typesetting in Garamond by
SetSystems Ltd, Saffron Walden, Essex

Printed in Great Britain by
CPI Antony Rowe

A catalogue record for this book is available from
the British Library

ISBN 978 1 84624 515 2

To Andrea, wife and mother

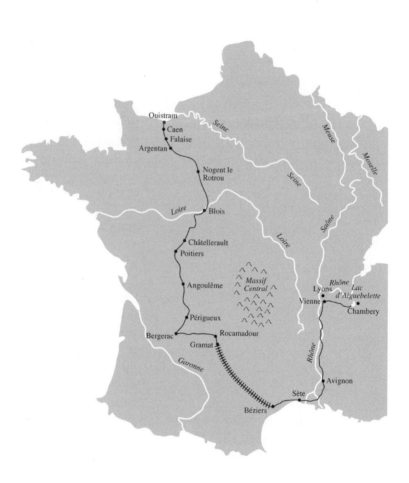

1 August 1997

DAY 1

Henley – Portsmouth – Caen – Falaise

It was 4.30 am. Caroline arrived on time. She had her son, my grandson, Toby, with her. He appeared, half asleep, with two soft toy animals peering from under his arms similarly seeming half asleep. He mumbled something about his mum getting up early and made straight for the stairs and to bed, which he knew well. A snuggle, a kiss and to sleep; he was settled in the room next to the au pair. The first stage of my proposed venture was successfully accomplished.

Losing a wife while still in middle age is not easy to cope with, particularly at special times such as holidays. I had observed others who had lost a dear one. Women always seemed to cope better. They invariably had the skills to look after themselves and the knack of establishing a social circle that provided a prop essential during the worst times of grievance. Men often seemed less equipped. Certainly that was true of me and despite my wife's advice in her last weeks on how I might organise my domestic life, cooking, washing, cleaning – all of it invaluable – I was quickly aware of my shortcomings. I was also not keen to become involved socially, particularly with those kind souls who felt it their duty to ask how things were and offer some sort of help. Outside my work and my immediate family, I looked for solitude.

This was the first summer following my wife's, Andrea's, death from breast cancer, a summer in which I felt more than a little desolate. I had carried on in as normal a way as I could throughout the previous year, but with summer holidays looming I knew I

1

faced a particularly difficult time. Holidays had always been special. The family had always looked forward to this annual foray with unconcealed expectation and even since the children had reached an age at which they could make their own plans, my wife and I had continued to make the best of these annual breaks. With my wife no longer present to make suggestions and carry out the preparations, it was now up to me.

I had considered several options. Perhaps it was not surprising that the strongest urge was to link my fondest memories of holidays with my wife and family with a major rowing event, and one taking place in France. In the early days, four children and limited finances meant that camping holidays in France had become a feature of our lives, with my wife, a former Queen's Guide, being organiser-in-chief. In the most recent years, as the children reached adulthood and more easily followed their own interests, it had been possible for my wife and I to enjoy the luxury of a French *gîte* or small hotel. There had also been occasions when we had travelled much further afield, following the exploits of our elder son, Terence, and the Great Britain team as they competed in the various world rowing championships.

On this occasion, however, I was planning a holiday which had a different ingredient. I had decided some time ago on the type of trip I wished to make. I felt that I not only needed a challenge but also the opportunity to learn things about myself that would strengthen me for the future. I had decided that cycling rather than driving would provide the right sort of milieu. I had figured that the equanimity likely to emanate from cycling in France would give me opportunities for quiet reflection and go a long way in helping me come to terms with my new situation. Although I had taken the view from the very first days after my bereavement that it was important to get on with life and not become absorbed in grief, I soon came to realise that a wound of this nature did not heal quickly. Simply going about my business of attending meetings and writing reports went only so far. I had to do something that would, on the one hand, help sustain the memories – and there were many – of life with a wonderful woman, while on the other help in coping with the hurt.

For this reason, the cycle ride was, I thought, a positive way of assuaging the pain of loss. The journey would also help me to place a memory of Andrea in a country she loved. I had decided that some spiritual reminder of our love for one another and our children, no matter how simple, posted in France, would be a fitting tribute. A lighted candle and a period of peaceful prayer seemed appropriate, especially as much of our life together had been centred on trying to help one another and our children to live out our Catholic faith. The lighting of a candle in a quiet yet beautiful church became my major goal.

A further reason, which had helped stimulate my thinking about the cycle tour, was the interest my wife and I had shared in rowing. The many national regattas, along with the World Championships and the Olympics, had become regular ventures for us, especially since our elder son, an oarsman of high quality who had represented his country at two Olympics, had been involved, and our contacts with the oarsmen, oarswomen and their families had blossomed. It had taken us to Western and Eastern Europe, Asia, the Antipodes and North America, and brought us a world-wide circle of friends. My hope was that savouring the atmosphere once more, especially with my two daughters, both keen and successful oarswomen in their day, along with my only grandson, would further contribute to the amelioration of the sadness of my loss. They, of course, were making their way to the championships by a different route and, sensibly, by car.

As with all journeys of this type planning was critical. By the time I started on what had begun to look more and more like an expedition, I had been planning for several weeks; the route, what I should, or could, take, how I would contact home if the need arose, and what physical preparation was required. My plan included carrying enough luggage and equipment on my person and the bike to allow me the option of overnight stops at campsites or in bed and breakfast establishments. I planned to be on the road for about a month.

I recognised the importance of having what might be termed 'good wheels' under me and, foreseeing the likelihood of some hilly and perhaps rough terrain, decided on a new mountain bike. I went for handlebars of the type we called 'sit up and beg' in my childhood days, as I had never mastered the art of drop-handle-bar cycling. Somehow, cycling with my backside in the air and my nose almost on the front wheel resulted in instability beyond my control, and so a classier model of bike for the French roads was out of the question. On advice from my elder son, Terence, I replaced the idiosyncratic wide, knobbly tyres provided for extra traction required by the genuine mountain biker with road tyres designed to give me a smoother ride. I had, therefore, a strong workman-like bike, capable of carrying a good load and withstanding the rigour of any conditions I was likely to meet. It also had enough gears to confuse a wizard. I borrowed a single-man tent of the crawl-in type from Terence, and added to my pack other essentials I thought necessary for my 'comfort'. I prepared as best I could for living a life full of anticipation and, not withstanding the main purpose of my journey, some anxiety.

As part of my preparations, early morning rides of about 10 miles or so became the norm and gave me fair warning of my limitations as a cyclist, particularly when shaken by the explosions of air created by passing lorries. The trips also warned me of the effort likely to be needed, especially when tackling the slightest incline. Never once, however, did I load the bike as if heading for the far beyond, and so did not challenge myself to riding fully laden. As I found to my embarrassment later, this was a mistake.

With the aid of well-thumbed Michelin maps collected over many years of camping holidays, and the *Michelin Guide to Camping*, I carefully planned a route to take me from Ouistreham, just north of Caen, down the West of France, along the Mediterranean coast and then northwards towards Lac d'Aigbuelette, to the east of Lyon. I reckoned, on the basis of all the advice I had received – there is no doubt you can always get plenty in the circumstances into which I was intending to put myself – that I should plan on covering between 45 to 55 kilometres a day. This was somewhat more than I was managing on my morning training runs, which were just about leaving me with enough strength to enable me to dismount without falling off the bike. I was still undecided whether I would cycle back to England after the rowing championships or hitch a lift. I had commitments that I might not be able to keep if the return by bike was likely to be too long. However, as usual, I was thinking ahead of myself as I wasn't totally sure that I would even reach my intended destination; but hope and the will are great motivators.

I had already prepared my bike and luggage for packing. Off had come the front wheel and the bike was standing ready for its journey alongside its neatly arranged accessories in the entrance hall. The dismantled bike and all my belongings fitted into Caroline's car surprisingly well and off we went – in the wrong direction! A quick turnaround sent us in another wrong direction. After 'calmly' discussing the situation, we eventually agreed a route. Portsmouth, and then hopefully France; here I come.

We reached Portsmouth by 7.00 am, well in time for the sailing. I looked at my daughter, my daughter looked at me.

'Are you sure, Dad?'

'Why not?' I answered with outward confidence.

What was going on inside me was another matter. Endeavouring to hide my nervousness, I did everything that was required, zombie-like, without realising fully what I was doing. I began to ask myself the panic questions I should have answered long ago when I was preparing for this journey in, what I began to realise now, were far from ideal preparations: 'Can I get the bike loaded without looking an idiot? Will I actually be able to ride it fully loaded? At what stage will I fall off? What will observers think of me?'

My daughter had pulled up directly in front of the queue of foot-passengers waiting to board the boat. There was no doubt that my arrival and subsequent actions helped them pass what would, otherwise, have been a rather boring 15 minutes. Amazingly, helped by my daughter, I loaded the bike with more ease than I had anticipated. I managed to slot the bike wheel back in place, fix the panniers and stack the tent and its accoutrements without difficulty. In fact I was quite proud of what I achieved, particularly under the gaze of the observing throng. But then, because of its weight, I began to struggle to yank the bike upright. Only Caroline saved me, grabbing the back wheel as the rear of the bike sought to slip away from my grip. She was on hand again as I tried to mount the bike by raising my leg over the side pannier, the tent and the sleeping bag. It was only with her help that I managed to achieve this task without falling over. I was disappointed there was no clapping among the watching crowd. Somehow, I managed to get to the ticket office and check in, hanging on to the bike, as Caroline, my support, disappeared into the distance.

The ticket attendant, hardly bothering to look up, told me to ride the bike to the boat – total fear! I looked old enough to know what I was doing, but I didn't know what was going to happen as I cocked my leg once more to get on the bike. The front handle bar tipped with the weight, the back wheel slipped, and I was hanging on with a leg on either side of the bike. Who was watching I do not know, but my discomfort must have been obvious. With a great wrench I managed to right the bike, get my posterior onto the saddle and find the pedals. I was off!

The ride to the boat across the flat tarmac went surprisingly smoothly and I was almost nonchalant as I approached the boat. Then, further anxiety!

'God, how do I get on the boat? Will I have to ride up one of the steep ramps to keep pace with the cars, some of which seemed to be finding it difficult enough? Where do I put the bike?' Will I have to unload all the gear for sailing?'

I was kept waiting at the foot of the loading ramp by a steward who didn't seem to give a cuss about what was going through my mind. Eventually he waved me on with, 'Walk up the ramp, cyclist!'

Having prepared myself for a challenge of tackling what was a very steep ramp, I was not sure whether this was a relief or a let-down. I quickly settled on relief, especially when I had my photo taken by a commercial photographer – as I was, seemingly, the only cyclist in residence – puffing, blowing and swaying with the weight of the bike. Once inside the boat I was left to my own devices. No guidance on where to put the bike, how to secure it or what to do afterwards. Somehow, I found myself on a car deck. I thought about standing next to the bike, and then realised I would have to leave the car deck once the boat was fully loaded and ready for sailing. Fortunately, I found a means of securing it next to a group of motorbikes, gave it a fond pat and headed for the lounge.

The first person I met on the boat was a rowing coach, sensibly travelling by car with his family, from a neighbouring rowing club back in Henley. We had coffee and discussed rowing, the common bond between us, covering topics such as the hopelessness of administrators, selectors, coaches we knew and even crews – in fact everybody but us. It was a relaxing time after the morning's adventures and one during which we followed with ease the age-old practice among sportsmen of setting their world to rights. At different points during this process we found space to exchange views about our projected journeys. His appeared somewhat mundane, but what I thought was his admiration, or it may have been concealed pity, for what I intended to do gave me something of a fillip.

I walked through the buffet bar, considering what I might have for lunch. As happens on Channel ferries, passengers head for the buffet bar in large numbers giving the impression that they are about to participate in their last meal. It seems traditional among holidaymakers to heap huge portions on trays. I could not believe the amounts people were piling up not once but sometimes twice, often with the comment, 'Eat up. We will not have another meal for a long time.'

On this occasion I decided to go expensive, recognising along with many of my fellow passengers that this could be my last meal for some time – or even ever went through my mind. I went into the upmarket restaurant, had a three-course meal, half a bottle of wine and coffee. An elderly couple came to sit next to me. They had a long debate with the French waiter about the menu, went through every offering and eventually ordered. About five minutes later they called the waiter back to change the order. What can one say about the English? The waiter's nose and upper lip twitched but his training was such that he kept his cool well. In French that I assumed meant, 'Of course, sir', he noted the changes and strode back to base.

We steamed into Ouistreham, a harbour my wife, I, and family had rarely used. Our normal landing and exit had been Cherbourg, a port in which we had been delayed for three days way back in the 1970s as a result of a French fisherman's strike. We had experienced three days of discomfort, rumours of what was likely to happen to 'Brits', and quarrels between disgruntled travellers which, in one instance, ended in a bare-knuckle fight. Tension produces strange reactions in humans! Now the problem I faced, which was producing its own tension, was how to get off the boat. I was given no instructions so stood alongside the motorcyclists with my bike at the ready. Too late. They roared off and left me standing. Cars began to follow and eventually I decided that all I could do was to follow the last car on my side of the boat as it moved off. I soon lost ground, as I was walking rather than riding, and I seemed to have been forgotten by the deckhands. Suddenly I had to take evasive action and just missed being mashed, rather like the potatoes I had been eating recently, as the ramp came down to let the cars off the upper deck.

That was not the end of my excitement. As I made my way down the exit ramp, being hooted by cars heading for the great beyond, I was enveloped in clothing, bits of paper and the paraphernalia one takes on holiday, as the boot of a car sprang open and the loosely packed contents came flying out. The driver's wife let out a scream, exchanged words full of expletives with her husband and, looking rather cross, appeared from the offside seat to collect what she could. I could not do much more than cling to my bike and peel off those parts of her underwear that were clinging to my bike and to me. I felt relief that the photographer was present only on boarding and not on disembarking.

As always happens when a ferry docks, cars, buses and lorries want to get moving as quickly as possible. They went speeding by me as I took my first dithering yards, or should I say metres, in France, all seemingly in the same direction. Some honked me as I adjusted a wobble, but in the main they sensibly gave me a good deal of space. My coaching friend sped past, waving his arm out of the window and shouting, 'Good luck'.

The journey to my first planned stop was Caen. I had hoped at one stage of my planning to build in a stop at Bayeux, a fascinating place that I had visited with my wife and grandson whilst on holiday in Normandy some years ago. Its historical content was an important element in all school histories for those studying the Middle Ages and the conquest of England by William of Normandy in 1066, later to be crowned King William I of England. My grandson was fascinated by the story and its representation in a series of coloured frames that showed much more of one of the most important events in English history than he had been used to in his primary school history book. This was the first visit for my wife and I also, and the memory of our excitement still lingered. Unfortunately, my route did not allow such a stopover and I progressed without having the opportunity to see once more the remnants of the most well known of 'tapestries' in England.

My journey continued without mishap to Caen. I had travelled through the town on numerous occasions on previous holidays, but this was different; I had time to observe. Caen still looked to me almost a new city. Badly bombed during World War II, many of its historical sites had been demolished. The rebuild has been done sympathetically. The planners had created a clean, modern town with first-rate amenities, whilst retaining evidence of its history.

The ruins of the castle, built by William of Normandy around 1060 and the site of many famous events including battles associated with the Hundred Years War, are still imposing, as are the two eleventh-century churches and the cathedral. Here and there are also houses from an earlier age. The modern town hall, very different in character, is, in its representation of twentieth-century architecture, no less impressive. On this occasion, anxious about my ride, my belongings and my first campsite, I did no more than ride through the town, but at the gentle pace of a cyclist.

For some reason my brakes had begun to screech every time I used them. Not surprisingly, as I travelled through this clean and well-planned town, I became the centre of interest at every set of traffic lights. At least those pedestrians crossing the road knew that I was trying to stop, but car drivers looked around anxiously to see what they might have flattened. Nevertheless, I persevered, trying on occasions to stop by putting my feet to the ground to slow down the bike and avoid using the brakes full on. However, I found that this practice presented the more serious problem of keeping the bike from slipping from under me. Being the skilled mechanic I was, I dismounted from time-to-time and looked at the back wheel, the source of the trouble, presumably in the hope that that would be sufficient to right the problem. No doubt my 'expert' investigation impressed any passers-by, but on no occasion did it impress the brakes. The screeching, the startled glances and the embarrassment had to continue despite my anxiety.

I left Caen with relief and headed to Falaise, something like 40 kilometres away according to my calculations. I had decided early in my planning that the minor roads were going to be my safest route and should also offer the most interesting rides. This usually meant extending the distance but on roads that I knew would be passable for cyclists. The journey went almost without mishap until I fell into the trap set by all continentals for unwary Englishmen. I only realised I had drifted on to the wrong side of the road when a car came round a bend, squealed its way across to the other side of the road and had to swerve back again to avoid an oncoming car. I carried on without quite hearing what the driver had to say. I guess the words for 'Idiot' are as recognisable in French as in English.

I reached a super campsite. Caravans, motor homes and tents, most seemingly self-contained, made up the clientèle. Campers consisted mostly of Dutch, French and English, with a smattering of other nationalities. My small tent made little impact and for once I could go about my business without distracting others. I unloaded with care, trying to ensure that I knew where to replace everything next morning. I unfolded the tent and began to wonder how the bits fitted together. I should have known, having had a small ridge tent in my back garden as a child when playing cowboys and Indians with my friends. My dad had always been around at that time of course, making sure that I did things properly. This was different and led to some scratching of the head and pensiveness before the first peg was eventually driven into the ground. As I grew in confidence, the hammer came up higher, the pegs went deeper and the tent took the shape I had expected. Soon I was unravelling the sleeping bag and putting the rest of my belongings tidily down the sides of the tent, ensuring that nothing touched the canvas and any rain was given no excuse to penetrate.

The town proved worthy of the evening visit I made in search of food. Set upon the banks of the River Ante, the town contains, standing proudly on a hill, the medieval castle in which William I of England was born. His statue dominates the main square, the military pose being a reminder of what I had learned of him when at school. Parts of the formidable former town walls also remain, enhanced by the more recent developments. As with Caen, much has had to be rebuilt as a consequence of the Second World War and the battles of 1944. The modern attractive shops and squares, which offered pleasant seating for pedestrians, gave the town a good ambience and suggested daily business which was not evident during this evening stroll. The French food and wine contributed to my feeling of well-being. This struck me as being a good start to my journey.

Even so, I could not get rid of my nagging concern about my brakes. I could not even find the French word for 'brake' in my pocket dictionary. As I crawled into my tent for my first night under canvas I had the awful feeling that my brakes would continue to harass me and also the good people of France.

I had decided before I made the trip to make brief notes of my daily ventures. I am not sure why. I certainly did not think of them being any more than a recollection of what happened, which would be a reminder to me and perhaps of interest to my children and grandchildren. Whatever the reason, this was the end of my first day and the beginning of my record, a record that I continued as I settled after each day's journey. I had paper, I had a pen and I began. Being a creature of habit, this was a practice that I continued each evening as I settled before sleeping.

2 August 1997

DAY 2

Falaise – Argentan – Sées – Essay –

La Chapelle Montligeon

Amazingly, I managed to pack the tent and the rest of my belongings as instructed by my son and fit everything into the appropriate bag. It looked neat and tidy and I surveyed it with pride. It looked less tidy once I had it on the bike, and I was aware that the balance of the bike was not as good as it could be. Nevertheless, I decided to press on. I had risen early and was concerned not to disturb those around me, a challenge that in earlier days the family of four children, close in age, would have failed to achieve miserably. I also had thoughts of the day ahead and how long it was likely to take me to reach my next destination, some 40 kilometres away.

I had loaded the bike without causing a stir and reported to the office to pay. For 16.5 francs this was not a bad stay. Still a problem with the brakes, but adept use of the nearside foot and crawling at slow speed down hills with a light touch on the brakes, easing them on and off, helped to alleviate my embarrassment for most of the time. Preparing my own breakfast had been beyond me on the campsite, especially as I had not found time to buy any of the necessary ingredients. But then, I had decided to live 'French' and so stopping at the first café for a typical breakfast was totally acceptable.

I cycled without mishap into Falaise and had *café au lait* and croissant. My Advanced Level French stood the test and I got what

I asked for. However, I didn't realise that eating genuine croissant without butter or jam was as challenging as one of those funny games we played as children when we tried to eat more of an apple on a string in a given time than our friends. We tried to eat so quickly that inevitably we found difficulty in swallowing, a problem I was having with my croissant. The coffee made the difference, but it was still a learning exercise to be remembered at later stages on my travels. The journey from Falaise to Argenton was mainly uneventful and my confidence grew. My only incident was when I mistakenly tried to pass off Swiss francs as French in a bar where I had a beer. Not surprisingly the barman was a bit gruff!

I found Argentan to be a well-kept town with flowers, pedestrian walkways and the fine church of St Nicolas. The town's history is reflected in the remains of a once-fine castle, which, over the past 800 years or so, has had to withstand English attackers on the one hand and the warring rivalries between the French nobility on the other. It still bears something of its history of a Roman town and of the medieval Benedictine monastery, but much has had to be rebuilt since the Second World War after its liberation by General George Patton and the US Third Army. Situated on the banks of the River Orne it offered an ideal place for a stop and light refreshment, which I enjoyed. My wife and the family had once stopped here and I remembered we got lost trying to get out. Things had not changed much and I was soon in difficulty. Thank God that I had learnt *à gauche* and *tout droit*. All the words in between meant nothing to me when a French woman began giving me directions, but I kept nodding and saying *'oui'* as though I understood perfectly. I had this experience of bemusement every time I wanted to leave a sizeable town, both with the voiceless road systems and the garrulous, but mostly incomprehensible to me, French.

It is strange that in eight years of French at school I was rarely expected to put together more than a simple sentence or two in the foreign language. I read Molière, Balzac and Alfred de Vigny, and I can make sense of a French newspaper, but the spoken word?

Forget it! One of the many improvements in the way our schools now teach languages is the opportunity teachers offer pupils to converse in the foreign language.

My next stop was at Sées, which is a lovely market town with narrow streets and shops exquisite for their individuality. And it was market day. The square in front of the imposing cathedral, the spires of which I had seen some kilometres away, was full of stalls selling typical French goods. Much of it was associated with eating and it was obvious that most of it had been produced by the local traders. There was a bustle about the place that was matched by the different voices, mostly with a joyful cadence, as buyers and traders exchanged banter. Both were clearly making the most of the day, and even to the casual observer they were not only bartering for the best prices but, so it seemed, sharing stories and gossiping about the events and people they had encountered during the previous week. For many, I suspected, it would be their one weekly visit to town and one of the few opportunities they would have to talk to others but their immediate family.

I ate in a very French bar in the square – mushroom omelette, green salad and a beer, mostly what I thought to be healthy eating. It cost 55 francs, which I thought was a fair deal, especially as I had four pieces of bread! It gave me the chance to leisurely observe the market scene. I was surprised at the array of vegetables, fruits and meats on sale. Somehow, markets in England have lost their rural flavour and people will travel miles in the hope of acquiring a cheap pair of Chinese slippers, under-priced coats, trousers and dresses, and only occasionally some genuinely farm-produced vegetables. In France, the markets I observed had remained primarily the centres for selling local produce. Fruit, vegetables and meat were in ample supply, as were home-made breads and cakes. Different stalls offered their goods for different prices and it was interesting to see how the different size of the queues reflected both the quality and the price. It was clear that the French women, because women were the main buyers, knew their market.

Whilst sitting in the café I reassessed my strategy for the day. It was clear from my map that my next camping site was not far enough to make a stop necessary. I was also travelling through pleasant rolling, slightly undulating, terrain, its fields characterised by the bundles left behind by already harvested corn crops. I decided, therefore, to pass through Essay, my pre-planned stopping place, as it would be only about 1.30 pm by the time I arrived and to go on to my next stop, La Chapelle Montligeon. I was surprised how well I was doing and the number of kilometres I was covering.

Even after Essay, the rate of my progress was making me wonder whether I would also be at my new destination well ahead of schedule. I was sufficiently encouraged to find time to make a stop at a bar for a beer. The half dozen or so locals who were already present followed my movements with interest, especially when I leant the bike against the wall and tripped over the pedal as I made for the door.

The bar had that dark and cool look that typifies such places in hot climes and it took a while for my eyes to adjust. As I drank a beer, my eyes fine-tuned themselves to being able to see what was around me. Bar life had settled back into its normal routine and I was able to observe without distraction. The lateness of the afternoon possibly explained what I witnessed. A couple, who were obviously not partners but enjoyed each other's company, were all but having sex at the bar; another chap who, by the deviations in his gait appeared to have had a few drinks too many, disappeared with a bottle; and an older one had to be helped through the door by his companions. Meanwhile, a baby was playing with a bottle in what appeared to a large dog basket, positioned on the bar. Before he left, another chap in true Gallic style went and kissed everybody three times, certainly lingering over women. He appeared to have enjoyed his afternoon drink, though not enough to give me a kiss.

The campsite at La Chapelle reminded me of the family's favourite site in Italy. Amidst trees, it was almost deserted and offered superb shower facilities. It was also big enough to encourage a walk to stretch tired legs. In the past the children had found such a location ideal for running hither and thither and would leave father and mother in peace for a pleasing length of time. What memories of a happy family those were and how I wished they would return. Only those who have lost the dearest love of their life can fully understand.

The town of La Chapelle Montligeon is about 96 kilometres west of Chartres and dominated by the ruins of the eleventh-century castle St Jean. Control of the town had passed between the English and the French during the Hundred Years War and in the sixteenth century it had been involved in the French Wars of Religion. In the latter, French Catholics battled with Protestants (primarily Huguenots and Calvinists) for supremacy, not just for their faith, but also for the political influence it would bring. Throughout the century war and peace alternated until some semblance of calm was eventually reached by the end of the sixteenth century. The town is graced with a superb church, Le Sanctuaire Notre Dame de Montligeon, which stands high on a hill and is visible as one approaches the town.

In our times, when the Catholic clergy are living through a period when criticism of their lifestyle is widespread, it was gratifying to learn of Father Bugeot. A nineteenth-century priest, he had been directed by his Bishop to La Chapelle, then a poor village providing few opportunities for its inhabitants. His desire to help led him into creating prospects of employment in printing and building. The main work of his ministry, however, centred on the creation of the Shrine of Our Lady, dedicated to praying for the holy souls in purgatory. This soon became a centre for pilgrimage, attracting pilgrims from all over France and further afield, set on praying for the holy souls passing through that period of purification that prepares them for the joys of heaven. It appears that only in the twentieth century has its significance waned, the outcome of what appears to be a changing view and seeming downgrading of purgatory within the Catholic Church itself.

On returning from my short walk and visit to the church I began putting up the tent only to find a wasp burrowing into the

17

ground on the very spot. I could not help but wonder if it had discovered a new line of attack. I need not have worried and never saw or felt it again.

Shortly after I had showered, a group of teenagers on those bee-buzzing motorbikes peculiar to France, and irritating to the English, arrived and began whizzing around the campsite. They seemed to have no care for other campers, of whom there were only a few, as they chased one another around and around, obviously seeking to demonstrate who had the fastest bike or the coolest temperament. My first thought was that they had come from the local town and were racing around, making as much noise as possible, just to irritate the campers, but eventually it was clear that they had come to stay. What joys were ahead? They pitched their tents amid shouts and laughter on the edge of the site.

The first warning of what was about to follow was a loud blast from what was clearly a 'ghetto blaster'. One of the youngsters started to sing, cheered on by his friends, and as the dark crept in, the singing became louder and the bursts from the ghetto blaster longer. By 10.30 pm a party was in full swing with loud, penetrating music and lots of cheering. I tried to sleep, but each time I felt like dropping off, I jumped at the disturbance of another encore from the singer. I looked at my watch at 2.20 am and the cacophony was still to be heard. I was surprised to be able to understand some of what they were singing and began to believe that my French was improving, until I realised they were singing in English. What a disappointment, especially as the racket went on and on. I could not help feeling that perhaps the motorbikes would have been better after all.

At last, the site went quiet and I, along with the other campers, no doubt, could settle to sleep. It was about 3.00 am. I had the idea of getting up earlier than usual, going over to the youngsters' tents and making as much noise as I could. This would have been sweet revenge, but it was never likely to happen.

3 August 1997

DAY 3

La Chapelle Montligeon – Rémelard – Nogent-le-Rotrou – Arrou

I managed to pack the tent and equipment quicker, if not as neatly, today. Not that it had been my intention, but it looked as though I would leave without paying. The site appeared to be unsupervised and so I made for the exit. As it was, the guy in charge suddenly appeared in the bureau. He was half asleep, his eyes bleary and his movements laboured. Nevertheless, he had sufficient of his senses to be able to do what was necessary to collect the tariff. He now insisted on filling in the forms which he should have completed on my arrival on the previous day in that painstaking way that is so irritable to the man on a mission. In addition, before he allowed me to leave he asked me to fill in a compliments book!

These things always give me concerns and I hate filling them in. As I flicked through this, it was obvious that previous visitors had enjoyed their stay, or were prepared to say so. I had learned long ago, as, no doubt, had some of those who had preceded me, that to write an honest assessment on an establishment which had been barely satisfactory could lead to an embarrassing confrontation with the owner or manager, while to be more conciliatory and give acclaim would do little to raise standards in the future. As usual in these matters, I chickened out, and wrote that I thought this was a nice place and that I had enjoyed myself. It would have been difficult to write anything else and escape from this burly looking gentleman, particularly as he peered at the page as I wrote. Whether he understood it I knew not but I was not about to take any chances. He seemed happy enough with it, even though he had done nothing to stop the 'music' or to give any sort of '*acceuil*', as the note on his door declared.

I left on a journey, which was relatively long, of about 80 kilometres to Arrou. The day started well enough in that I had prepared for breakfast by buying an apple pie and chocolate bun the previous evening. My increasing expertise in packing my belongings and loading the bike, plus my quickly eating what I would have liked to describe as a 'healthy-food breakfast', allowed a speedy getaway on this Sunday morning, a day on which other campers did not seem to rise early. The bike was holding up well, a good investment it seemed, and for some reason the rear brake went quiet. I could now enter a built-up area with head held high, so long I did not touch the front brake too often.

Much of the riding was straightforward and I exchanged waves with several groups of real cyclists. On one occasion I had to ease off the pedals because I thought I might catch up a single cyclist who was loitering ahead. I was desperate not to appear too serious about my cycling on this venture. Fortunately, he turned off in the next village, leaving a two-year-old as the only cyclist that I had passed so far.

At Mass that day I had found the time for prayer and for thought. It is surprising that the one seems to blend into the other in a way that I sometimes find disturbing. I find concentration in prayer for more than a couple of minutes, for instance, very difficult and soon find my mind wandering, distracted by events recent and past. Similarly, when in private thought I slip into short prayers without being aware as to why. On this occasion I had no problems with concentration. I prayed with what I hoped was sincerity for my wife and for my family and gained much comfort from my thoughts on the sacramental bond that had given us so many happy years together. I left the church somewhat more contented than I had entered it.

I managed coffee at about 10.30 am in Nogent le Rotou. Nogent is typically French, with a nicely situated bar overlooking the square in front of the Eglise St Hilaire. I was tempted to visit the church and also the Château St Jean, dedicated to Joan of Arc and, incidentally, to years of war between the kings of England and France. But I knew I had some distance to travel and I did not want to stretch myself too much. After all, I had had plenty of warnings from my children about what I should and should not do on this journey, and one of them was that I should not try to cover too many kilometres on a particular day. They foresaw, I think, the likely consequences on the next. It was enough, therefore, to find a comfortable seat and enjoy a cup of coffee with a croissant, this time with butter, to help while away my mid-morning break, and observe the French arrive at, and depart from, the café, clearly enjoying the coffee that was to start their day. Then it was time for my own departure. I managed to buy two apple tarts and an Orangina which would have to do for a cyclist's lunch.

I found the ride to Arrou enjoyable. The sun had emerged and warmed the air through which I was travelling at no great pace. I began to have that feeling of well-being that I always felt in France, with warm sun on my back and the gentle pace of life associated with holidays. With few cars on the road I had the opportunity to look left and right at the ever increasing fields rich in sunflowers, the fruit trees or those bare corn fields, stripped of their lushness by the combine harvester. The occasional family preparing their picnic lunch in the shade of the trees did nothing to disturb the bliss that I was experiencing on that gentle ride through country lanes and small villages. Eventually, I found a quiet spot beneath trees for my lunch of apple tarts and Orangina. Here I could settle and lay back to enjoy the peace and relative quiet, and to think.

So often in the past the world had opened its doors for my wife and I as we left the ferry and drove through Cherbourg, Calais or Boulogne on the summer's adventure. The key was always to get south of La Rochelle, where it seemed that the weather brightened and the charms of France enveloped us. Then we could say we were on holiday. The children looked forward to the pleasures of campsite play, mixing with children from other countries and testing the warm waters of sea or river, while mother and father were in eager anticipation of resting beneath blue skies. The long days in the sun were often interspersed with visits to places of interest, sometimes at some distance from the campsite if there were none in the immediate locality.

It is strange coming away from home on my own. It helped to become engrossed in daily routines. Most of the day I managed because there were things to do – packing a tent, cycling, looking for routes, searching for food and walking slowly from A to B. On occasions, time was the enemy. It may have helped to hunt for places of interest at my quiet times in the day but I hesitated because of the uncertainty as to my eventual destination and what I was likely to find when I arrived there.

Inevitably, there were times when I wished I was at home, a feeling exacerbated by the French Sunday, especially at lunchtime. The French linger over lunch, which seems to take an age. Families then seem to find ways of entertainment, sometimes home based, such as playing cards, or that was the impression I had from a number of the village households I passed, or go off to the pool or picnic areas to share their pleasures with their children and others. Witnessing it now, and with memories of what I had seen in the past, I wondered what I was doing living in a field in a tent and having little sustenance for the day. Almost inevitably I asked myself, 'Why didn't I stay at home?'

But then I also remembered with a startling clarity that on this occasion I had come to France for a special reason. I remembered Andrea and how her passing had left a house of sameness and emptiness, one that bore her presence but one in which, inevitably, loneliness pervaded. It was a strange sensation, one which was becoming all too common to me, to feel an emptiness creeping up on me when I saw family gatherings with joyful children, fathers overseeing their play, contented mothers looking on, or couples walking hand in hand towards me or simply talking with one another, particularly as it was not that long ago that I had enjoyed such pleasures.

These thoughts had also occupied me in Mass that day. I thought of how Mass had seemed a weekly challenge at one stage of our lives, loading four very young children into the car for church and with the expectation of yet another 'embarrassing' experience during the service which almost inevitably followed. These included my son trying to douse the Mass sheet he had accidentally managed to light with his Easter candle, the angelic smile of a young altar server kneeling by the altar and the growing pool of water extending from under his cassock as he looked angelically heavenwards, and the swapping of seats by the children as each moved first to their mum and then, with less enthusiasm and usually because they were being a nuisance, to their dad. Attempts to hush the children to quietness during the homily were always a trial. These, and many other stories, became the topic of amusing conversations within the family as the children grew older, when times had been better and no one had foreseen how things were to change. This unforeseen change was the reason for my being at Mass on my own in France. It was also the reason for the fervour with which I prayed that day.

It is not easy to forget almost 40 years of marriage, how it had started and how it had developed. In particular how it had ended, with my wife in my arms as I sought to keep her lips moist with drops of water and her mind alive by whispering in her ear. All the children were also present in that late afternoon in July, all aware that there would be no recovery. Once the eyes closed and the breathing stopped, the very being of my wife departed and the body seemed to have no purpose. The tears and deep sadness eventually came as the children realised what had come to pass, but only in moderation in light of our sad expectation. Each individual present in the house that evening would need to find his or her own way of coping, sometimes within the family and sometimes on their own.

Such memories quickened my resolve to reach my destination

and light that special candle. Dreaming came to an end as I stood, pulled up my bike, almost skilfully on this occasion, and continued on my salving journey south. Arrou was my destination and a good dinner my expectation.

The campsite at Arrou is well kept and has good facilities, though the French never seem to know how to use WCs, seeming determined to leave them looking as though they are being well used. Even so, they represented a better challenge than the 'feet in the snow' I was mostly finding and which left me with wet feet and sometimes more. The lack of loo paper in most of the camp toilets presented another problem that I felt I had to solve as soon as possible.

I was looking forward to dinner but discovered all the restaurants in Arrou were closed. This seemed unusual to me for France on Sundays. A shopkeeper told me there was a restaurant in the next village. I thought she said it was a kilometre away. Sadly, my Advanced Level French failed me again; it was three and I had decided to walk as my bum was by now too tender to cycle another kilometre. Of course, the restaurant was closed and so I had to manage on a beer to slake an ever-increasing thirst. Back the three kilometres to Arrou with some mad French teenagers leaning out of a car window waving and shouting me a fond '*bonjour*'; or at least that is what I thought they shouted. Another beer in Arrou to get over the walk, standing up of course, and that was my sustenance for the day.

I solved the loo paper problem on my walk back from my search for an afternoon meal by raiding a public loo, even though I did not need to use it, and availing myself of pieces of paper. I had to make two attempts, as the loo was occupied on my first sally. I had to make a second attempt looking somewhat desperate so that my real intentions were not discovered. Once inside, I stuffed my pockets with loo paper and quickly exited. I was on my contented way again with only a slight feeling of guilt, only to find the campsite loos had been replenished in my absence. The Michelin guide is not renowned for nothing.

Crikey, as I was sitting writing, a group of teenagers with guitars walked past. Surely, not another midnight concert! The musicians walked past me again, but in the opposite direction. 'Is this a sign of hope', I wondered.

As it was, the night passed without incident. I was getting used to sleeping on the ground, which always seemed to have the bumps in the wrong places, particularly around the thigh area if I tried to sleep on my side. The sore bum and aching thigh did not disturb my sleep on this night, as I was determined to compensate for the excitement of the previous evening. The tent offered cover, the sleeping bag was warm and the rucksack a reasonable pillow, so what else did an intrepid camper such as I need?

4 August 1997

DAY 4

Arrou – Châteaudun – Beaugency – Maves – Suèvres

One thing about starting off on the first of the month – it is easy to keep a record of the number of days one has been away. I had planned a quiet day today with only a 20 kilometre ride, but I was doing so well that I decided to carry on to the Loire, 40 kilometres beyond my original destination. I had my usual apple tart for breakfast – with a bottle of water as there seemed to be no coffee in Arrou – and set off on a 60 kilometre ride. As usual, I started with what might be described as enthusiasm, especially as I was now getting used to the saddle, having found the best way to sit, and was finding riding becoming more comfortable. The road was mainly flat and, believe it or not, this was the first day of real sunshine, encouraging me to resort to sun screen. The fact that the sun shone made me feel much more like a real cyclist, as I was able to get down to T-shirt and shorts, but I still looked far different from the guys in the Tour de France.

I had come intending to spend some time camping and some time in cheap roadside hotels or bed and breakfasts. This had influenced what I carried on the bike. I had taken advice from my son, who did a fair bit of cycling now that he had finished his rowing career. Strapped to the front of the handlebars was a square cycle bag, containing the odd tools such as spanners and a puncture outfit, as well as those things for which I needed ready access, including razor blades, shaving soap, toothbrush and paste, soap, and a towel. There was just enough space for the odd piece of fruit and sweets for the journey. The bag was topped by a transparent

26

cover which enabled me to slide the map for the day between it and the top of the bag, thus providing me with the opportunity for viewing my location at an instant and avoiding directional misadventures – or so I thought. All this was neat and tidy and, to my mind, indicated a well-organised traveller.

The rear of the bike was something else. Two panniers hanging from the rack over the back wheel contained most of what I thought I needed and had been advised to bring for the journey: on the one side clothing, including pyjamas and a change of shorts, underpants, socks, shirts, wet weather needs and a sweater; on the other side I carried what might be termed the needs of the camper. The best advice I had was to carry at least a small stove with fuel, (though I remember using this rarely), matches, a couple of small saucepans, plastic plates and some cutlery. There was no place for food, drinks or for those unguents that had been so essential on family holidays in the past. The drinks bottle found itself attached to the frame of the bike, as was the normal practice among real cyclists.

Somehow, even when I had become more used to packing for the bike, I never seemed to get the two panniers to balance one another or to look as tidy as the cycle bag at the front. The imbalance was to some extent righted when I strapped the tent and all the rest of the camping accoutrements on the rack over the back wheel and panniers. The tent, inside a bag containing pegs, hammer and guide ropes, was at the base. The groundsheet and sleeping bag were placed above and both were topped by plastic sheeting. They were strapped down with several bungee cords. It did not take long for me to realise that unless the strapping was done very carefully the balance of the bike could be badly affected as the tent moved from side to side and the plastic sheeting began to blow in the wind. I tried several ways before settling on what I thought was the most practicable, as each time I had packed in these early days the outcome caused me some embarrassment. A slip to the left forced me to adjust my steering to the right and one to the right forced an adjustment to the left.

The locals watched the seemingly drunken cyclist tortuously winding his way through their villages in amazement. Wrestling with the bike at every stop had men and women ready to rush to help me keep my balance. Eventually I solved the problem by ensuring that the tent was central and any other tools that were inside the tent bag were evenly spread left and right. This seems obvious to the observer, I suppose, but it is not easily done, especially by a joke cyclist such as I.

The one bit of advice I didn't get was to bring shin pads – there are dozens of different ways a bike can find to inflict pain around the shin area. My worst experience was at a picnic area when I tried to stand the bike against a post, missed and the pair of us ended up in a heap. In the process the pedals scraped my shins. I yelped and carried the scar for the next few days. I tried unsuccessfully to disentangle myself from the bike and get to my feet but it was only with the help of a woman who was having a quiet fag away from her car that I succeeded. She saw my predicament, helped me to my feet and provided further support as I struggled to get the bike back on its wheels. I had several other marks indicating how well the bike struck out during this process. I think the woman escaped unscathed, but I think her fag went for a burton.

Talking of fags, the French seem to enjoy rolling their own and then chewing them rather than smoking them. Time and again, old and middle-aged Frenchmen would light up and then chew the cigarettes until they were mushy paper in their mouths. Only occasionally did they seem to puff, timing it to perfection to keep the fag burning.

Once back on my bike, the gentleness of the road gave me time to think about the advantages and disadvantages of the different modes of travelling. Cycling, other than giving a sore bum (and now sore shins), seems about the best to me. Cars go further and faster, but you live in a box and hardly make contact with nature or people. Walking is fine, but it takes a long time for the scenery to change. Cycling gives you the freedom to look around, smell the scent of different fruits and flowers, from time to time speed, especially down hills, and keeps you close to other people. Lots of French people wave and shout '*bonjour*', something I had not experienced when driving. The French also appear to have more affinity with the cyclist, unless I am confusing, in my case, affinity with amazement.

My journey continued well and I had no doubt that I would easily reach my new and more challenging target. Then, misfortune struck. For some reason my watch strap broke. Fortunately, I caught the watch as it was about to fall off my wrist and it was not damaged. However, it had to go into my pocket and I was reduced to telling the time by the sun.

Despite my more casual approach to the ride I still seemed to be arriving at places long before I had expected. I reached my first port of call, Cloyes-sur-le-Loir, in good time but was gasping for a drink, the result of the heightening temperature. At the far end of the main street I saw umbrellas going up and felt in luck. I reached the café, stationed my bike and sat at a table. After ten minutes I realised the café was closed and the sign said it would not open until evening. The umbrellas were obviously a gesture or the work of an over-zealous waiter.

I decided to mosey down the street, found a paper shop and saw maps in the interior. I needed one of this region because I did not have one in my map armoury. Sod's law! The only Michelin not on display was '*numéro* 64'. I picked the next best map and stood in the early morning paper queue. When I reached the front with quite a tail behind me, I took a chance on asking if the shop had '*numéro* 64'. The lady disappeared down the shop to where I had been looking for '*numéro* 64' and then went into several cupboards. The other shoppers were obviously delighted having their daily routine disrupted! Wonder of wonders she found '*numéro* 64'. I was in business for 18 francs.

Next door I bought an apple tart and an Orangina and then made the mistake of asking the way to Fréteval. Three women started talking at once – a bit like my daughter-in-law and her

29

seven sisters – and the only one who was not part of the conversation was the guy with Advanced Level French. Eventually a decision was reached and instructions given. I think I understood three words – *usine, gauche* and *Morée*. Fortunately it was enough to get me moving in the right direction. I wended my way onward along the main street with some trepidation, turned left, followed the signs which directed all but local traffic to the right and then picked out the factory some 200 metres down the road. A little further on I saw a sign pointing to Morée. Relief! My understanding had been better than I thought, though it is fair to say that the route had not been that difficult to follow. Once I reached Morée, my map came into its own.

The ride was uneventful and I reached the campsite near Suèvres in good spirits. I was amazed at what good progress I had made. I was conscious that the scenery was changing, something that we had always become aware of around the Loire Valley when we had been travelling by car. The crops seemed to be changing, with more fields of sun-drenched sunflowers, now waving their heads in welcome as I passed, though I may have imagined it, rather than the fields further north which were seemingly unclothed once their crops of corn and maize had been harvested.

The campsite, Le Château de la Grenouillère, was impressive. It was clean and hospitable, though somewhat expensive when compared with the other sites on which I had stayed. The amenities were designed to attract long-stay holidaymakers rather than the one-night cyclist. The name was appropriate, as at one end of the site was a small, attractive château. In addition, an open-air and an enclosed swimming pool provided plenty to do for children and adults, whilst other attractions included table tennis, a bouncy castle, pedal cars for hire and so on. The arrangements for eating were also first-rate and I was able to get a substantial meal once I had set up the tent. To my delight, the loos were of the highest order, clean, well-maintained and modern. There is little doubt that for the family camper who wanted to have all his needs administered to in one place, this was an ideal location. For me, pushed with my little tent into a small corner of the site, it had the feel of a secure unit in which I had been condemned to solitary confinement.

As for the journey, I felt I had had a good day. But in relaxing I felt my shins. They were scraped red rather being cut deep enough to bleed and they needed some attention. I administered some ointment that had been recommended for cuts and bruises before I left home and trusted to its healing powers as I prepared for another night under canvas. As I relaxed into my sleeping bag I began to feel that I was enjoying my experiences more than I had expected.

5 August 1997

DAY 5

Suèvres – Blois – Chaumont-sur-Loire – Chenonceaux

I left Suèvres, another of those small ancient towns which seem to pepper every part of France, with little opportunity to explore. It was a place that I hoped some day to return to and enjoy what it has to offer more fully. I cycled in sunshine and made my way southwest to the River Loire and Blois. The morning was pleasant, and brought back many fond memories of previous trips along this most beautiful of rivers. Unfortunately, as the day wore on clouds began to threaten. By the afternoon, after I had progressed some way down the Loire Valley, it began to rain fairly heavily and curtailed what could be done. Fortunately, I had reached my destination at Chenonceaux and had just set my tent before the heavens opened in earnest. It meant I spent the afternoon part sleeping and part reconsidering my strategy instead of visiting the castle and the nearby town of Amboise, which also boasts a castle and other medieval buildings.

Earlier in the day I had enjoyed the ride by the Loire, an impressive river with great views across its bridges, especially at Blois. On my journey I passed some superb châteaux. At Blois, the former seat of the dukes of Orleans, the dominant building was the church. It could be seen clearly above the streets, as it proudly mounted the heights of the town seeming to leave the many attractive, bustling streets below to those with more mundane intentions. The stretches of woodland on the eastern approach roads and also to the west of the town added to the spectacle. I left with a dramatic memory of the town that had once been at the forefront of French history. The Loire had always been my favourite river journey, even when driving alongside it with four lively children on the back seat in years past, and this experience did not disappoint me.

One of the secrets of taking young children on long journeys is knowing how to entertain them so they do not distract the driver, or his wife for that matter. I never found the solution. In the days before hand-held DVDs and other technological aids that seem to provide a part solution these days, we often resorted to such activities as 'I spy' or competing as to who could collect the most of a chosen number from the registration plates of passing cars. The best solution, however, was for the children to fall asleep, which was always a possibility for mine on long trips. Then, peace reigned. My wife and I could make our way blissfully along the roads, broad and narrow, without a care in the world, quietly chatting about the countryside and the plans for the future days on holiday. The payback came of course when the driver stopped for a restful sleep himself. Children woke up, were often grumpy, argued and became downright unruly, preventing that restful bliss the driver had been dreaming of. Such memories came flooding back as I pushed my way along: fond memories as it happens.

This turned out to be one of my great days. I actually passed another cyclist! I must say I hesitated with a sort of embarrassment before doing so and hung some distance behind, rather like a rider in the peloton in the Tour de France, watching his every move, hoping he was going to turn off down some side road. Why I should be so concerned I am not sure, but I had in my mind that if he were passed by a cyclist of my appearance, with a bike with squeaking brakes and an ungainly rear luggage rack, his morale would be seriously damaged. In the end I had no option and smoothly overtook him, cheerily shouting '*bonjour*'. If nothing else, the incident seemed to suggest that my cycling legs were getting into gear; that was until I saw that he was about twice as old as I was!

The road at this stage was quiet and offered little opportunity for a stop and a drink, until I saw a small inn ahead. Its sign read *Fermé Mardi*. It did not look promising as this was Tuesday, but I was much in need. As I approached I saw *madame* and decided to chance my arm. In my best French, which did not add up to much, I ordered a coffee. *Madame* obviously recognised my need, affirmed she was closed but could do me a *café au lait*. Not only this, but she also had a croissant that she was happy to let me have. I could not thank her enough, especially as she did not ask me to pay, and I sat at an outside table enjoying the refreshments and the sun, which now seemed to have settled into its regular daily exercise of appearing in a cloudless blue sky, which is what the English expect of the sun in France. It was while I was drinking my coffee and enjoying the rest that the cyclist I had passed earlier went by.

I sat a little longer than I would normally, hoping the cyclist would disappear and save me the embarrassment of passing him again. It was not to be. Once in the saddle I was on his tail in a few minutes and with a cheery '*bonjour*' cycled past him again. Nothing in his demeanour indicated that he cared one jot.

Now I am the king of cyclists; I have my brakes fixed! I had eventually reached a town in which I spotted a cycling shop. Again relying on my limited French, I endeavoured to explain to the owner my problem with the brakes. As soon as he had grasped the problem he was on the job. Demonstrating the professionalism that I lacked, he had screwdriver in hand in seconds. He loosened, exerted pressure and had the brakes fixed in about two minutes. He charged me nothing for the adjustment and sent me on my way wishing me well. I could now cycle with gay abandon, approach traffic lights without fear and enter towns downhill without distracting the citizens.

As the afternoon wore on, the clouds appeared and thickened and drops of rain began to disturb my equilibrium. The rain increased in intensity and forced me to stop and don my anti-rain gear. I had not expected this and hoped that the inclement weather would soon depart. This was not to be. The rest of the day's journey was interrupted by flurries of rain that grew in intensity before I reached my destination.

Fortunately, the campsite, a three star, was run by friendly people. One lent me a pen to write with as my own had refused to write, and another lent me a cloth to rub my bike down after the rain. Thirty francs were also knocked off my emplacement but it was still almost 20 francs for the night. This reflected the popularity of the Loire and the prices that could be charged by camp owners.

Having arrived in teeming rain I was pleased it had eased a little while I was putting up my tent and organising my equipment, though it and I still got soaked. The joys of wet camping!

Once my bed for the night was established, the rain, which had now abated somewhat, continued to enforce a period of inactivity, and I lay looking through the door of the tent. Before long I was studying rather than just looking. I soon realised there is a campers' walk. Head down, shoulders drooped, casual flat-footed gait, the camper seems to be looking as though he is going nowhere in particular. This is very obvious when he is making for the loo with bits of loo paper sticking out of pockets. Loos are not campers' favourite places and it seems that the longer it takes to get there the better. The stride certainly quickens as the camper heads back to base. Of course, caravans usually carry their own and so their owners often walk with a different air, one which indicates contentment and, for some, the look of superiority. Not surprisingly, they rarely walk in the same direction as the real campers, that is in the direction of the loos, and often seem to give an impression of disdain for those on the ground.

My own visit to the shower today was an experience. The rain eventually stopped, the site resumed its buzz, and I thought it wise to get to the showers before others could. One of the secrets of pitching a tent, I had found, was to be near enough to the loos to be able to reach them quickly, while being far enough away to avoid any unpleasant odours. Having made my entry and being in a hurry I headed into the first shower. To my dismay I realised I was in a shower for the disabled. This was not too embarrassing once the door was closed and I could not be seen. There was certainly plenty of space too. Unfortunately, before I had a chance to organise myself for a shower my soap spun out of my hand, zipped across the floor and passed under the door into the corridor. Disaster! Dare I leave it there? Had anybody seen the moving soap? Would somebody think the disabled person had come to some harm and send for help? With all these thoughts racing through my guilty brain I decided I had to chance it and make a sortie out to retrieve the soap. I put my towel round my waist and non-chalantly strolled out to pick up the soap, bumping into two teenagers in the process. I picked up the soap and limped back into the shower.

I had only just completed my 'phew', turned on the shower and stepped under the water when I found I could not now lock the bloody door. The size of the cubicle was against me. I couldn't hold the door shut and at the same time have a shower. On the other hand, if I tried to have a shower the door swung open. If I could not find the answer I was likely to be discovered and earn the reprobation of my fellow campers. How could I make such a mistake in the first place and then not check to ensure that I was safe? Also, why did I not just change showers? As it was, more and more people were entering the shower corridors and banging doors shut as they found and entered a shower, thus making it more difficult to exit without being seen. Despite the steam from the shower, I at last found the locking device, something a little special for a disabled toilet, and was able to lock the door, saving myself from any further embarrassment. I waited until all was quiet in the corridor and then slipped out, limpless and quick, and made it back to my tent.

Once clean and dry and with the rain stopped I ventured into the nearby village. Despite the threat of further rain, I found a pleasant seat on the terrace of a café overlooking the river. To my astonishment, a couple with a monkey came in and sat opposite me! I was staggered but nobody else seemed to mind. The monkey happily ate nuts and then shared in titbits from its keepers' dinner before disappearing under a napkin as if to say cheerio. I have sat at home eating in the garden with my own cat chasing frogs and birds, and I have become accustomed over the years to seeing the French take their dogs into restaurants, but a monkey was something else. One German woman took photographs from every angle and a couple of children had to change places with their parents so they had a better view of the monkey. It passed through my mind that I would have been quite happy if they had all found some reason to go to another restaurant, but in reality I found the episode amusing and one unlikely to be repeated in an English restaurant, where even dogs are not allowed.

By the time I arrived back to my tent it had begun to rain again and this increased as I struggled to take off clothes, put on pyjamas and crawl into my sleeping bag. I was now hoping the tent would continue to live up to its billing. The pitter-patter of rain on the tent was not as comforting as I remembered it on the window at home when still young, and I lay there listening as it increased in intensity. My anxiety was not eased by the thought of the bike being out in the open, presumably getting sodden as would be the odd bits and pieces still attached to it. The tent survived the night, though children, seemingly talking in their sleep in the next emplacement, didn't help me get much sleep through the night.

I was disappointed that I had not had the opportunity to explore the small village of Chenonceaux. Situated on the right bank of the River Cher it boasts the beautiful Château de Chenonceau, which is distinguished by being built across the river, its several arches giving access to boats. The classical turrets and the grey-white walls topped with the darker grey roofing, viewed from a distance, represented the typical French château well. It also had the distinction of providing habitation for Catherine de Medici and Mary Stewart (or Stuart as some would prefer). The village also contained some interesting buildings from a bygone age.

6 August 1997

DAY 6

Chenonceaux – Blêré – Loches –

Descartes – Châtellerault

Next morning everything was wet on the outside, but the tent had done its job and prevented me and my belongings from suffering the worst of the wet weather inside. Nevertheless, it had left a shivering dampness that pervaded everything. The exterior of my sleeping bag and some of my clothing had the feel of having been put through the washer but not been given time to dry. They felt squidgy, unpleasant to the touch on a day that offered little hope of their being dried in the warm air of the France I thought I knew. Accepting that the dull morning did not convey the promise of a brighter day, I did my best to find some clothing that would not tease my skin too much with its encircling clamminess and headed for the shower. My expedition, because that is what going to the loos sometimes feels like when camping, was fortunately less adventurous than on the previous day. Oddly enough, on this occasion, I did not feel that a shower was going to make much difference to me.

The prospect of another ride in rain was not encouraging. I had become somewhat pessimistic as I packed my damp and sometimes sodden belongings. Not surprisingly, they seemed to take up much more space than on the previous day and I was aware of their being heavier as a result of the moisture they retained; I had to push and squeeze to get them into the appropriate pannier. I felt that things couldn't get much worse – until I pulled the zip to close the pannier bag which contained my spare clothing. Whether I pulled too hard in my frustration or the bag was too full I am not sure, but the zip just flew off the end leaving me with no means of closing the bag. As one does when one feels a bit miserable, I let my shoulders droop, looked skyward and muttered under my breath. I hoped and believed that this would be just another straw, hopefully the final one, on a day that had not started well. Then I pulled the zip on the tent bag – lo and behold – this flew off the end as well. I couldn't believe it! Together, these incidents presented me with a predicament; problems to be resolved during the day, but, I resolved, not at a time before coffee.

The bike loaded and the site cleaned up, I proceeded to the camp office and small café to settle my account and find some breakfast. The person who served me had just bought the site and was hoping for success. She was Dutch and talkative in that very good English that most Dutch people seem to have. I have always been intrigued by their skills and ruminated on the techniques they use to learn English. I have never yet met a Dutchman with whom I could not hold a sensible conversation in English. I reflected on my own talent in languages, and the unsuccessful efforts that I had made to master the skills. It suggested that those who guided my learning had not hit the right buttons, whilst those in Holland were forever finding the right keys.

In this case, the owner explained that she and her family had often camped in France. 'We have always enjoyed the French way of life as we have seen it and so my husband and I decided to leave Holland behind and settle here.'

'Why a campsite?' I asked.

'Dutch families looking for the sun of southern Europe spend their holidays camping. We were one of these. We learned quite a bit about camping, and so the obvious thing was to take on a campsite.'

'But was this not a risky business?'

Rather philosophically she replied, 'New ventures are risky but we are better fitted for this than probably any other undertaking.

We know plenty of Dutch people likely to use it and stray Englishmen like you just add to the fun.'

It was clear that this was a family concern. She, her children and her husband seemingly did most of the jobs about the site – cleaning, reception, shop assistant and chef. Fortunately, I found in her what I was finding in lots of people on my journey; an empathy with the cyclist. Her kindness extended to letting me have a coffee and croissant free of charge. We chatted about the campsite's prospects, about the habits, good and bad, of campers, and the good start to the season the site had made. Eventually, I wished her, her family and her enterprise well and set off on my way.

I knew which direction to take, but was less sure of the site I would stay at. My original itinerary was in shreds, as I was covering far more kilometres a day than I had anticipated. This meant that I had to refer constantly to my Michelin guide to pick out sites of reasonable quality. It also disappointed me somewhat that I had not taken a little more time to look at those places of special interest that I had passed on earlier days.

The day remained cloudy but the ride was relatively straight-forward. I reached Loches, an interesting market town. It was market day and busy, with stalls and sellers offering much to buy. There were also small artisans' shops in the side streets able to sell or repair a whole range of things from clocks to candlesticks. This looked a good place to attend to my luggage and find a means of opening it. I thought it sensible to try the tourist information centre. They spoke reasonable English and advised me where I could find a *horloger* and a *cordonnier*, either of which might be able to help me.

The instructions sent me through the middle of the market and the bustling crowds, a place not suitable for a bike with panniers and tent. After earning the occasional and sometimes brusque '*oui, oui*' or something like it to my, '*excusez moi, s'il vous plaît*', I decided that I needed to duck down a side street if I was going to avoid an international incident. Not surprisingly I was lost in seconds and had no idea how to follow the instructions of the helpful tourist agent. But by chance, I found an ideal *cordonnier*. He was helpful, interpreted my French beautifully and once he had seen my problem set about solving it. He had just the right equipment and attitude to deal with my difficulties. He fixed the zips and produced a new watch strap. The latter had limitations, but meant I could keep an eye on the time. He and his assistant, who may have been his sister, were the sort of skilled artisans that one fears are in danger of extinction in England. I wondered where I could have obtained, in what once was the workshop of the world, such immediate and high-quality service.

My ride took me through some beautiful villages. When I first went to France in the 1950s and 1960s, the French seemed to be little interested in gardens but now they take great pride, not only in their gardens, but in their villages. The shows of flowers were magnificent and village after village illustrated how well, in my eyes at any rate, they compared with the typical English country garden and in several instances offered more. They had not yet captured fully what might be called the English lawn but I could only be impressed with the geraniums, roses and the abundance of other flowers I saw.

The other interesting aspect of this journey was the helpfulness of the French I came into contact with. I had a completely different impression of the French from that I had gained in the years I had travelled by car. They willingly helped me when I was in difficulty, were communicative, as far as was possible with my limited French, and viewed me more with interest and amazement than suspicion. I suppose the chances to get to know one another when travelling quickly from A to B by car leave few opportunities to establish any sort of relationship. It also seemed to me that the French responded differently to foreigners than the English. Where we are reticent and perhaps seem a little arrogant, they are more open and willing to help. Of course, this may be simply the difference between being a cyclist and a car driver. Also I had the feeling that while we tend to speak to foreigners louder, believing this will help them understand, the French seem to speak quieter. Neither strategy is a great success!

The thing about cycling, which I was now getting used to and having to reflect on, is the different emotions it gives rise to. The exhilaration of going downhill is usually quickly followed by desperation at the sight of the next climb. Often, one gets a sight from a distance of an undulating road, the climbs always seeming to be steeper than the dips. As each obstacle is overcome, the cyclist gains satisfaction and the encouragement to continue. Somehow, the road seems to draw the cyclist onward and encourage him to do more than he should.

My route took me on to Descartes, 'I think, therefore I am' country. Initially called La Haye en Touraine, the town was the birthplace of the philosopher René Descartes (1596–1650). The town was renamed La Haye-Descartes in 1802 in his honour, and then renamed Descartes in 1967 to cement its links with the great man. The narrow winding streets of the town provided an attractive sojourn, giving me some time for a beer. The statue of Descartes commanded the space in front of the town hall. I was deeply impressed, having superficially studied Descartes for a paper on the history of political thought when reading for my degree, and I took my time over the beer. Cars, however, continued to twist and turn in their anxiety to reach their destinations on the thread-like street before the statue, oblivious to my thoughts and seemingly of those of the great thinker.

Having arrived at Châtellerault earlier than expected I knew I needed to reconsider my strategy if I was going to reach my final destination at the planned time. My thinking was also being influenced by the fact that there were mountains ahead. The fear of the mountains had been with me for some time. To date I had conquered all the hills that the roads had placed before me but I knew, mainly from my observations during the Tour de France, that mountains were different. On one occasion, whilst driving with my wife up Mont Ventoux, a classic Tour climb, I had inadvertently taken the part of the road that a sole cyclist needed to use to maintain his impetus as he snaked his way higher and higher. Despite his obvious fatigue he still managed to make his thoughts known to me, but continued on and I assume, and with the empathy of a fellow cyclist indeed hoped, made his way to the summit.

But the weather was also causing me consternation. It had started to rain again during the afternoon, though not heavily, and it looked likely that it would continue through the evening and well into the night. My concern was how to keep my belongings dry so that I had something to wear on the following day. I had not anticipated so much rain and although I had taken some precautions when preparing for the trip, I knew that I did not have enough spare clothes to cope if the rain continued. Fortunately, by the time I reached the campsite the rain had stopped. This gave me hope for the future and certainly the opportunity in the present to rig my tent and arrange my belongings in such a way as to keep them dry if it rained again in the night.

Campsites vary widely, not only in facilities and clientèle, but also in the make up of the soil into which pegs have to be driven. In many respects, the latter is far more important than the quality of the facilities. On this particular site I should have been more attentive and well warned when the owner suggested I took a site which was 'less' rocky than the ones used by caravans. A rocky site can be a disaster for campers; the effectiveness of their pegging makes the difference between whether they are sleeping under a tent on the following morning or not. I looked around until I found what appeared to be a likely site, one which seemed to contain less stones than most and began to secure the tent. I managed to get the pegs in about an eighth of an inch. My hands were sore from pushing and guiding the pegs between the stones which were just below the surface. Each time I used the hammer, the pegs bent and flattened as if to say 'No way, mate'.

By the time I had finished the tent was tenuously pinned to the ground. If any sort of wind blew our way the tent was likely to become dependent on my own weight and that of my belongings to forestall disaster. My other concern was that if it rained again –

it had fortunately abated while I was settling in – the loosely fixed tent, with a tendency to sagging, would gather water rather than shedding it, begin to wilt in the middle, make contact with some of its contents and with increasing intensity splatter its occupant with raindrops. I had to hope that the weather would be kind overnight – some hope! But I have camped enough to know that there are limits to what can be pegged into rock – and the camper meets the problem long before the mountaineer.

As I finished hammering, an intrepid Frenchman asked if he could borrow the hammer. He added to his armoury a large stone in case he needed a replacement weapon. Shortly after he had returned to his emplacement there was banging, what I took to be swearing in French, and the clear sound of the squashing of pegs hitting the ground as they refused to go through rock. Having suffered myself, I thought it would be interesting to see how someone else might be faring. I nonchalantly wandered over to see how he was doing. To be fair, most of his pegs appeared to be at ground level, but on closer inspection they had only pierced the soil by the same amount as mine. In truth, they had been beaten into a variety of shapes and angles. He seemed happy enough with his work, though I was not sure how he would peg out on the following day with so many bent and misshapen pegs.

After eating a reasonable meal at the campsite restaurant I took a stroll round the site. There is no doubt that there are occasions when caravans look the ideal camping accommodation. They provide secure cover, a reasonably comfortable bed and enough water and electricity to allow decent meals to be cooked. In good weather, caravaners can sit out in the sun, often shading under a suitable awning, and in bad they can retire into their dry caravan. They also have the advantage of having their own loo. Certainly, they looked the right sort of accommodation this evening as the clouds gathered, but I recognised that I was unlikely to be able to pull one behind the bike! Fortunately, the clouds did not turn to rain that night and those in tents were no more disturbed by bad weather than those in caravans.

7 August 1997

DAY 7

Châtellerault – Poitiers – Availles-Limouzine

Having camped just north of Poitiers, I was reminded of the statue of the Black Prince in the square in Leeds. He sits there proudly on his horse, sword drawn and threat in his posture, commanding both respect and awe. I first saw it as a child on a shopping trip with my mother and I was young enough to be much affected by its charisma. This was a prince who had fought and beaten the French and the sort of 'hero' we learned about in history in school in those days. Since then of course, the approach to, and interpretation of, history has changed markedly in schools, and I wonder how the Prince is viewed by children today. Some would no doubt be surprised to hear that his connection with Leeds depended on no more than the whim of an early twentieth-century mayor who believed the city centre needed a statue of presence and used his own money to ensure that it had.

No matter, recalling his exploits so close to the city associated with them brought back many childhood fantasies of great men and brave deeds. I could not pass Poitiers without being reminded of the campaigns he and other English nobility waged in France. As far as I know, and, I think what I was taught in those immediate post-war years, they raised their armies on the promise of, among other things, pillage and rape, or something similar. It staggers me how they did it. Even now, you can travel miles through open country in France without a hope of pillage or rape, so what it was like several centuries ago, before the rise in the birth rate, is mind boggling. I will also need to re-read my history to find out how

45

these armies, if that is what they were, travelled on their stomachs. There must have been days of searching for food and trying to find what limited amounts of pillage and rape were available. I can only think they relied heavily on their imaginations.

The previous evening I had a passable meal at the campsite at Châtellerault, and spoke for a while with the waitress who was a law student in Poitiers. Her English was about as good as my French, but we fell into a mode of conversation I have often noticed with the English and French. She spoke in pigeon English, interspersed with French words, and I spoke in pigeon French, loudly, using English and arm waving when stuck. Why we didn't or don't just stick to our native languages and rely on signs or facial expressions, which is what we do most of the time anyway, I don't know. It is highly amusing observing others conversing in this way and I suspect our conversation was no less enthralling to the other customers.

She was enjoying her course. The law in France was different to that in England, she said, and tried to explain some of the variations. We soon discovered that this was unlikely to get us anywhere so stayed on more mundane topics such as why she was working on the campsite.

'It is essential,' I construed, 'to work in the summer months because of the cost of the course and the need to pay for my keep.'

'This is also the case in England,' I replied. 'Many students find work during the summer.'

'Although this has its drawbacks it also has its compensations, such as meeting someone as interesting as you.'

I preened at this and let her go on, believing that I was understanding very well.

'I have always wanted to go to England, but meeting an Englishman with whom I can converse is the next best thing.'

For no justifiable reason the conversation made me feel good and I made my way back to the tent in better spirits than I had left it.

After packing the following morning I went for breakfast, pleased that I had booked this because it was still raining. I was hoping to meet the same waitress but there had been a change and the morning waitress was a no-nonsense French speaker, more in the style that I had been used to in earlier days when holidaying with the family. If I didn't understand what she said, that was my problem!

The route I had planned for that day was a mistake, despite the fact it passed through some beautiful countryside. The map had several < > signs, an indication I soon learned of rises and dips in the road. I should have known better when preparing my journey. But how pretty the River Vienne and its environs are. I could understand how the tree-lined river had attracted the wealthy to live near its banks. Noble families from England are said to have châteaux in this area and it is not surprising. Several stately-looking homes I saw are unsurpassable in their beauty, with grand entrance gates, magnificent approaches and those always seemingly sun-topped turrets that distinguish French from English country houses and castles. I was reminded of these when working in Romania's capital city, Bucharest, aptly named 'Little Paris'. Many of the pre-communist buildings were modelled on the French style, largely a result of the influence of France in Romania at the turn of the century. In the years since 1950 much had been done that destroyed the beauty of the city but post the revolution in 1989, money was again beginning to flow into Romania and much of it was being invested in restoring Bucharest. Reawakened pride looked again to what was left of the French influence, as banks and other companies of importance in the new economy took the lead in resuscitating once beautiful buildings.

By lunchtime the sun was out and the sun lotion on. By the time I had climbed a few hills and the perspiration was pouring out of me I began to wonder whether cycling was a good idea or whether I should have stuck to going by train. Some of the hills went on and on, round bend after bend, giving me the impression that there was no semblance of parity in terms of length between those that went up and those that went down. But I was here for a reason. The loss of a wife is hard to bear and it seemed to me that I had been in danger of thinking that now that the children had left home and I was on my own the world was too empty a place.

The danger of beginning to feel sorry for myself and thinking that there was nothing in life worth living for was real. This was not the only thing that gave me motivation. I could not escape my wife's living spirit, even though she had now passed away. Her determination to overcome difficulties was immense, and never more so than when she realised that her cancer was terminal. When the hospital decided they could do no more for her and allowed her home, she was determined to sleep, as was normal, upstairs, no matter how difficult she found the climb. Almost to the last, she went up on her knees, praying the 'Hail Mary' step by step as she did so, becoming more dependent on my support as the days passed. It was having shared life with such a spirit that encouraged me to be positive after her death and respond to the new demands of life. This journey was a sign of that response as well as a dedication to Andrea.

The journey down the Vienne valley was full of delights. Potted plants such as petunias and geraniums decked the garden walls, bridges and roadsides through the villages and all were a blaze of colour. This afternoon was a French summer at its best, displaying those features that attract tourists from England and the rest of northern Europe.

It was while admiring what was around me that in one garden I saw a woman sitting sunbathing, surrounded by, of all things, model geese. There were few villages that I had passed that day that did not have their ducks, geese and hens, but they were of the moving kind. But model geese? I was still trying to work out what she was seeking to achieve by the time I reached the campsite.

The campsite sat beautifully by the side of the Vienne. Although it did not live up to its Michelin billing completely, it came close. It had a good range of amenities and had the advantage of being close to a pretty town.

The site was busy and appeared to have been taken over by

pétanque players. Everybody seemed to be playing *pétanque* when I arrived and I soon learned there was a competition, seemingly the explanation for the shouts and groans. I used to enjoy playing *pétanque* on my previous visits and had, in fact, bought a couple of sets so that the family and I could entertain ourselves in quiet periods on the campsite. I watched a little before heading towards the area for tents.

I was shown my emplacement, but as I started to unload my bike I was set about by two dogs from under a caravan. They were pretty stroppy and would not be appeased by first my calm reaction, 'good dogs, good dogs' and then my more aggressive '*Allez, allez!*' The campsite manager, having ascertained the situation and no doubt being slightly amused, at least that is what the look on his face suggested, returned a few minutes later and suggested I might like to move. I said '*Bonne idée*' and collected my belongings and moved across the way.

I was in the process of flinging a few small stones away and setting up the site when I realised four *pétanque* players were taking a keen interest in what I was doing. One asked the obvious, in French of course, 'Are you putting your tent up?' – or at least that is what I thought he said. They had obviously just finished their game and were going to report in but found my antics more interesting. They exchanged a few more comments, none of which I understood, and were clearly having some sort of laugh at my expense, so I threw in the bombshell, '*Qui a gagné?*' I got some reply in guttural French and off they trooped. I know the guy who had asked what I was doing didn't win because a little later I saw winners being given bottles of wine. My man carried only his boules under his arm.

I am a man of little pride. When in a mess I don't hesitate to share it. The day's journey had been arduous and I was having visions of another day of riding up and down hills. And so I had the bright idea of going to the tourist office and asking for the easiest route to Périgueux. The tourist officer understood my dilemma. He took my map and with his finger traced out a route that took me on to Confolens, then Angoulême and finally Périgueux. He said that this was a ride of gentle terrain and pleasant countryside, with some choice stopping places on the way, such as Brântome. I had planned a trip of over 100 kilometres, the outcome of the lure of the road and possibly my growing confidence. I trusted his judgement and set my mind accordingly. Little was I to know what was in store for me!

8 August 1997

DAY 8

Availles-Limouzine – Confolens – Angoulême – Mareuil

The morning ride was particularly tough for me. The visit I had made to the tourist office in order to make sure that I made the right decisions about the route to take did not seem to have paid off as I began to head towards the Dordogne. The young man fortunately spoke English and was able to point out what he described as an interesting route which would help me avoid the worst of the traffic. He knew enough to explain that the road to Périgueux would be hilly at the start but after not too long a time would become flat all the way to Angoulême. He was wrong on one account and it is not too difficult to guess which. I don't think he had ridden to Angoulême.

When you have hill after hill you are encouraged to keep your head down and concentrate on the road. Viewing the road from such close proximity gives the opportunity to study a range of things that do not normally concern you. For instance, one is keenly aware of the changes in the surface of the road throughout a day's ride, and the effect such changes have on the cyclist. The smooth tarmac gives a feeling of singing along, whereas the rough pebble finish leads to the cyclist fighting for every yard. There is a range of surfaces in between these two extremes, each with its distinctive level of resistance. I came to wondering to what extent road engineers tested their finish on bicycle wheels.

The other aspect of interest is the nature trail. I suspect every local species of bird, animal and reptile could be identified on the road, the outcome of their unfortunate contact with car or lorry. I saw the remains of different types of birds, large and small, black, grey and white – crows, thrushes, pigeons and finches. Rabbits were also plentiful and a young fox had been unfortunate enough to stray in front of a vehicle of some sort during the night or early morning. A snake had also failed to make it across the road along with several hedgehogs. This was rarely the sort of thing one noticed in a car, especially speeding along on a largely empty road such as this, and I was further reminded of how limiting the experiences were when travelling in the 'box'. The main aim always seemed to be to get from one point to the next, usually as quickly as the speed signs allowed. Admittedly, there were stops at interesting places on the way and the local atmosphere sampled, but I was learning that this did not compensate for what I was experiencing. Environmentalists of all kinds would have been delighted with the very little damage my cycle was doing to nature.

This was the day when I realised that I was a ragamuffin among cyclists. Cyclists take a pride in their dress – above the crossbar wind-resistant, tight-fitting lycra all-in-ones, brightly coloured and sporting favourite drinks or the names of champions and their teams, capped with protective headgear set at a serious angle, and below, cycle shoes specially designed to ensure grip when sliding into pedals. It is true that my washed-out green T-shirt, baggy shorts with turn-ups designed to offer more of my legs to the tanning sun, trainers and soft floppy hat (needed because my protective helmet had let the sun through, which had led to painful sunburn on the head) worn beneath my helmet gave me an air of distinction. Certainly, my garb distinguished me from real cyclists. Nevertheless, I always managed to get a cheerful '*bonjour*' from any that passed me. It is not surprising that I remained envious of their smart appearance and their obvious dynamism, particularly when grouped like the peloton in the Tour de France, throughout my trip.

My day's journey was made harder by getting lost on my approach to Angoulême. It was a sod! Instead of taking the southern direction on the ring road as I arrived, I gaily passed the turn-off and found myself on the north circular, heading westwards and towards Bordeaux. I had to work my way round the west side so that I was going south on an extremely busy ring road. I met some very steep hills before reaching the south of Angoulême and the road to Périgueux. This aberration added at least 24 kilometres to my journey, led to some hard riding and proved very frustrating, especially as it was in the hottest part of the day. What should have been a fairly straightforward ride to my next campsite became a test of endurance.

I was disappointed not to be able to go into Angoulême, as I had read something of its history. Described as a small city, a thousand years old, it is said to have an old town centre with interesting churches and buildings. It would have been a good spot, it seemed to me, to stop, relax with a beer and a little lunch, and then do a quick circuit of the sights. Unfortunately, it was not to be.

The day settled once I had left Angoulême behind and I was able to concentrate a little more on the sights. I had set myself a long journey, however, and so I also needed to think how I was to conserve my energy. My ride took me through open land, small villages and onto tree-lined roads such as that through the Forêt de Dignac. I enjoyed it, finding shade from the sun under the firs at one stage and then benefiting from its full glory the next. The dappled road led me through feelings of contentment that one can rarely experience in the car. For this holiday I had made a choice which was different and I felt I was getting some benefit from it. There was no doubt that I was having the time to think and gain a better understanding of my new situation. The fact that I had taken this alternative of a cycling tour against the advice of some set me to thinking about free will.

I have often, as I have grown older, contemplated the significance of man's free will. The more I have read, the more confused I have become. God gives us the freedom to make choices, yet when we face adversity we pray for His intervention and when we have something to celebrate we thank Him for making it possible.

The line between the operation of free will and God's intervention has become more and more blurred to me, especially since – as is the case with all the believers I know – we all pray for His intervention. Admittedly, those of us in the Catholic Church are taught not to expect that His intervention will be as we desire it or even as we might recognise it, but we are taught to believe that if we ask in true faith He will respond, and in a way that will be in our best interests.

One of the main reasons for my journey was to give me the opportunity to work through this conundrum and help me understand how my wife's and my prayers, and I am sure those of many others on her behalf, have been answered as they have. I suspected I would not find the answer to this question on this trip, but it is a mystery that I needed time to explore. Like so many people in my position the constant question had become 'Why? Why us?' Such a question had, to some extent, influenced my prayers. I did not really expect to get the answer in this world, but I knew that there was something about the question that encouraged me not to lose faith in Christ's promises to us. Indeed, because of what I had been taught about my prayers not always being answered as I would wish, I was prepared to accept.

When I arrived at Mareuil I had little difficulty finding the campsite. It was very quiet and the man in charge was clearly disappointed with the number of campers. He welcomed me and suggested a good place for pitching my tent. This seemed superfluous in view of the emptiness of the site and the limited likelihood of many other campers arriving. However, I took his advice. I pitched my tent knowing that I would be making some small contribution to his income and made my bike secure. I then headed for the village and some sustenance.

The village was an attractive place and had enough people to make the local hostelry lively. It offered good opportunities to mingle with traditional French life: an attractive bar, talkative customers, shaded seating and the warmth of a balmy evening. To cap it all, I was soon aware that the road was full of cyclists, of the type that look like cyclists, and that they were about to start a training spin or something more serious.

The bar clientèle didn't take much notice initially. The cyclists set off with the usual hub-hub, some joking with one another, some calling to avoid other cyclists, and others with the serious looks of likely winners or newcomers to the scene. I eventually realised that they were involved in a race and that this was the start of the warm-up session. After the cyclists had done two circuits of the course the starter held out his flag and waved them on into the race. I watched with eager anticipation and decided I would try to pick the winner.

No doubt there were marshals at key points, such as the one placed outside the bar. Each time the cyclists were about to pass, he whistled a warning to any other road users so that they could take appropriate avoiding action. It was not long before the competitive nature of the exercise became evident, as by the third circuit one rider had made what I think is called in cycling terms 'a break' and several others were beginning to get left behind. However, as cycling enthusiasts know, a group of riders in the peloton make small beer of a single rider and by the time the cyclists passed again the lone rider had been overtaken. Nevertheless, the race was generating a fair amount of excitement in the bar and as the leaders swept past on each circuit the drinkers began to cheer. Inevitably for such a road race, non-racing cyclists, cars and caravans had become intermingled with the racers, creating problems for the marshals and not a little danger for the cyclists. One of the reasons, as I understand it, for this form of road racing not being seen often in England.

By now I had chosen my favourite and watched him carefully as he went by, lap after lap. Two groups of cyclists eventually broke from the peloton and among the leading one was my man. It was from these groups that the winner emerged. I was disappointed to see that my man was third. He had worked hard, but, I felt, not quite as hard as I had on that day. The race just finished in time, as it was getting dark and the riders had no lights. Throughout the race excitement, the bartender had continued to serve assorted drinks, especially to a group next to me, and had clearly done good business. Some of the customers had also done good business, as money changed hands, clearly the result of betting on the places achieved by different riders. I had enjoyed the evening, had a reasonable meal and drink, and happily wished the patron well as I made my way back to my tent.

9 August 1997

DAY 9

Mareuil – Brantôme – Perigueux – Bergerac

One of the things I have always admired about real cyclists is their apparent ability to do almost anything on a bike. They can ride without hands, bend down and do and undo toe clips, turn almost 180 degrees to see what is going on behind them, collect food and drinks and consume them; they nonchalantly take out their water bottle, throw their head back, drink and replace it, all at a time when they are working to keep pace with other riders. Cycling in heat makes this last skill most essential, especially if you don't want to be stopping every five minutes to quench a growing thirst. It was the skill I realised I had to work on with some commitment as I was now becoming so confident on the bike. Through my regular procedures at the beginning and end of a session, I could at least get on and off the bike without falling over (mostly), and I could take a hasty look over my shoulder when the need arose. I had not yet, however, conquered the water bottle. All it needed now, I thought, was confidence. I had tried several times before but had failed miserably, never actually getting down far enough to touch the bottle or to exert any pressure on it.

This had to be the day. I had watched the race the previous evening and admired the skills of the riders who made it look so easy, bending, reaching, unclipping, withdrawing, drinking, and then replacing without any sign of a wobble on the bikes. Surely, with my growing expertise on the bike, I could achieve something similar. As the heat was increasing the further south I went, the more important it became to be able to drink at will. I was carrying my bottle in the usual place for a cyclist, that is in a holder attached to the front strut of the bicycle frame. It was no distance to reach down, but, as I had found it, needed secure control, if not bravery, if I was to get the bottle out of its holder, to my mouth and then back into the holder with the grace expected of a real cyclist. I waited for a quiet bit of road and then snatched the bottle out of its holder. The bike wobbled but the first task was accomplished successfully. Now the classy bit – head back and water squirted into my mouth to give me that refreshing feeling. Cap clipped back in place and all was well – until I tried to get the bottle back into the holder. Would it go? Would it hell! The bike wobbled and I was on the verge, brakes full on. I had failed the second part of the exercise with almost disastrous results.

My next attempt was a few kilometres down the road. Again, all was quiet and all seemed safe. The routine went as well as previously until I tried to replace the bottle. This time I missed the holder completely, caught its edge with the bottle, which loosened my grip so that when my knee came up with the pedal and made contact with the bottle, it went spinning into the middle of the road. Again the bike wobbled to a screeching halt on the verge, and I had visions of my water bottle following the experience of the birds, snakes, foxes, frogs and rabbits. Somehow it survived as it spun around in the road and before it could be crushed by passing vehicles I managed to retrieve it. I then had the problem of getting the bike back on two wheels so that I could continue on my way. I endeavoured to do this looking as unconcerned as possible. Believe it or not, I continued to practise. When one faces 3-kilometre hills in blazing sun, without shade, one risks a lot of things. Sufficient to say, as the day progressed I improved to the extent that I could snatch a drink and replace the bottle, but I did not reach that smooth flow of bending, straightening and drinking that I had observed the previous evening. I consoled myself by remembering that I had a pack on the back of the bike and this was the reason for my apparent ineptitude.

It seemed a long way to Bergerac, especially as the route was plagued with hills. It was a hard ride. Not surprisingly, I took stops more often than on previous days and took the opportunity to take in fluid as often as I could. I came to the conclusion, on the basis of the amount I consumed – water, Orangina, beer – that it takes more to keep the human engine going than it does to keep the mechanical engine on the move. I got to thinking how far I got on a bottle of coke – in one place it cost 15 francs – and how far a car would get on the same amount, cost-wise, of petrol. I worked it out that it cost me well above £5 for the 100 kilometres I had covered and I suspected a car would do it cheaper. It is amazing what you think about as you tackle a hill 3 kilometres long marked with the fateful > on the map.

One of the pleasanter aspects of the day was my visit to the small but delightful Brântome. It was a village recommended to me as worth a visit and I was not disappointed. Described by some as the Venice of Périgord, the combination of water and active streets certainly gave that impression. It offered tourists the calming Jardin des Moines and the tranquillity of the abbey, as well as the busy streets with their variety of shops, bars and small cafés. The coffee I enjoyed gave me the opportunity to observe what appeared to be the world on holiday.

The campsite was two star and full because I was now in holiday country – French in large numbers, British, Dutch and German. Because I was a mere cyclist with a tent and not a driver with a caravan of one sort or another, I was given an emplacement with others of similar ilk by the side of the river – it had the feel of a happy young colony in which I was the old man at the party. My particular site was a pleasant one and overlooked Bergerac on the other side of the river. Once the tent was pegged I quite enjoyed looking across to pick out the main points of the town, about which I did not know a great deal.

I discovered that Bergerac is a fascinating town but one with too many attractions for me to see in the short time I had planned to be in the area. This was one of the limitations of the type of journey I was on. It would have taken me two or three days to absorb what it had to offer, and with a deadline ahead of me I did not think such a delay, pleasant as it might be, could be justified. The range of restaurants, people and streets made my wander through the town a pleasant one. I enjoyed what I saw and made a mental note that on another more favourable occasion, this was a town that I should not miss. The half-timbered houses from a bygone age, now refurbished to serve a different generation of people than the one for which they were built, fused naturally with more modern structures and appealed to me as they always do, no matter what town or country I am in.

As in many areas of western France, the town's history became a blend of English and French as the kings of the rival countries endeavoured to establish supremacy during what became known as the Hundred Years War. There is no doubt that the English kings of earlier times had an impact on the development of towns such as Bergerac but little remained of their influence. French towns have a character of their own and one which is quite different to that of an English town. The turreted buildings and noticeably sloping, gabled roofs give the French towns that rather picturesque look that one often associates with children's fairy stories, whereas the matter-of-fact buildings of most old English towns, attractive in their own right, suggest a much more materialistic approach to life. Even the beautiful thatched cottages of the Cotswolds do not hide the fact that business was at least as important as beauty to the English.

I was pleased to spot what I thought was a quiet café along a side street. I entered and ordered a beer and a sandwich. As I looked round I realised that the café attracted a very mixed clientèle – some knew the waiters well, two or three women looked more than casual drinkers, and there was a little scenario of race relations when a couple of bully boys made what appeared to be unsavoury comments at a group of coloured youngsters sitting at a nearby table. I had heard that there was some racism in France, but this was the first time I had detected it. The café certainly offered variety.

I wandered back to the campsite intending to have an early night after my exertions of the day. Once I reached my tent I took time to look around and I realised that across the river an open-air production, under lights, was in full swing. I remembered that I had seen some posters referring to Count Bergerac and realised that the activity was concerned with his exploits. I was too far away to follow the story but the play was obviously going well judging by the laughter from the audience wafting across the river towards us.

On our side of the campsite things also began to warm up. The corner of the site on which I had pitched my tent was obviously the meeting place for the younger campers. As evening drew in they seemed to be attracted to the spot like bees to their hives. They brought their own bottles with their varied contents and different items of food. As youngsters do they naturally drifted into a circle, took their places and mostly sat with crossed legs. They clearly represented different nationalities, occasionally speaking the language of their birth, but they conversed, interestingly enough, in the common language, English. It was fascinating listening to the exchange of stories and the adventures they had had. Dutch, Germans, French and Danes talked of the towns they had passed through, the sights they had enjoyed and the experiences they had unexpectedly encountered.

Most were hitch-hikers, some were travelling by train or bus interspersed with walking, but none was a cyclist. I wasn't invited to join, as they probably realised I wouldn't have a bottle or much else to offer, and that I was an 'oldie' likely to be somewhat out of place with the rest. Whatever they really thought caused me no concern as I sat in front of my tent on the edge of the group, participating in spirit. I imagined that such groups often came together at the end of day's trek to drink, talk and sing, meetings that added to the richness of this kind of holiday, and I suspected that there were particular campsites that lent themselves to it. This was certainly one.

Eventually I tired and decided to go to bed. It was a pointless exercise as the talking and singing went on for several hours. Oddly enough I did not feel as upset as I had when similarly disturbed back in Chapelle Montligeon. These were genuine campers, determined to enjoy themselves; the songs had a charm about them which reflected the different countries from which the singers came and several of them I could hum to within the confines of my tent. As the evening turned into night some of the revellers were clearly the worse for wear and before I fell asleep I remember wondering how they would feel on the next day.

10 August 1997

DAY 10

Bergerac – Couze-et-St-Front – Alles sur Dordogne

As this was Sunday I decided that it should be a quiet morning, giving me the opportunity to attend Mass in Bergerac. I had picked out a church the previous evening, and so I was able to go straight to it without the worry of having to search the town for one or travel in the hope of finding one en route. I found Bergerac to be an interesting town when explored on the quiet of Sunday morning and even more appealing than I had thought it on the previous evening. I could take time now to look more closely at some of the buildings and the architecture of earlier centuries. The charm of the quiet, narrow streets, typical of medieval towns, and especially so of many French towns and villages, brought a calm, which was ideal for a Sunday morning. The window boxes full of flowers in bloom, red, pink, blue and yellow, and the wooden shutters, more for show than purpose it seemed as some of them hung precariously from their iron staples, created a warm friendliness that I had not always associated with the French. Other buildings were imposing and I looked at them with awe; the museum of religious art, for example, and the Eglise St Jacques.

The statue of Cyrano de Bergerac also stands proudly in the town, though it is said that he spent little time there. His name lives on, however, bringing renown of some sort to the town and adding to its reputation, which has also been built on fine wine and beautiful surroundings. By the river the open-air theatre was set up for the drama of *Cyrano de Bergerac*. I was reminded of the previous evening when my distant observation of the play had

63

eventually given way to a younger generation that was more interested in sharing their own stories of the world than in hearing about the exploits of the character, more fiction than fact, created by Edmond Rostand. I must say that I was impressed with what I saw on this Sunday morning.

The congregation at Mass reflected that of many others in France and most other countries I had visited. A good many people were beyond middle age, the only young members of the congregation being with their mothers and occasionally with their mother and father. Mass in a French church follows the same ritual as that in England, and as that in any country that I have visited where Mass was celebrated, but it feels different and has some features that are purely French. The presence of a *chanteur*, for example, generates a different momentum to that in a Mass in England and the movements of the congregation also vary; sometimes the congregation stood when I expected to kneel and sometimes sat when in England I would have been standing.

There were also a couple of interesting scenarios that I could not help but notice on this occasion. The *chanteur*, standing at the side of the altar and having the task of leading the congregation in the singing, clearly had difficulty communicating with the organist. Despite his exaggerated nodding of the head, the organist failed on occasions to pick up the signal with the result that there were a number of false starts. The congregation was obviously used to this and coped with it admirably.

Even more noticeable was the middle-aged lady who sat in the front row. She had walked past me when I was tying my bike to the disabled sign, and caused a bit of a stir in her big blue hat pulled to a jaunty angle, blue-spotted almost evening-style dress, blonde hair, dark glasses and swaying hips. She did not enter the church by the nearest and most convenient door but swung her way with style to the massive front door. From there she then walked the length of the aisle followed, as I am sure she had hoped, by the eyes of all. When she found her front row seat she took out at least three different prayer books and prayed throughout the

Mass with seeming great reverence. The style of the entry was repeated at the end of Mass as she left and I had no doubt that the scenario would likely be repeated Sunday after Sunday. For my part, my own contribution to the proceedings was for once less striking but no less obvious to the old lady taking the collection – I had no francs to put in the basket!

After Mass I returned to the campsite and prepared for my day's journey. I was looking forward to riding along the banks of the Dordogne, a river that Andrea and I had enjoyed viewing from the car and discussing on several occasions as we ventured into different parts of France for our holidays. I was now something of an expert in packing away the tent and other trappings associated with my stay and of loading the bike so that it did not wobble too much. I was hoping for a ride along a flat river-bank, recognising that there would be a few twists and turns, but believing that rivers like the Dordogne tend to meander in summer along wide and relatively flat beds. The early part of the ride was welcoming, if not, as I found out later, a little deceiving. It was mainly flat and I was able to pedal at my own pace for the first time since the early part of the tour. The Dordogne looked beautiful and the road followed it close enough at this stage to give some superb views.

The bright start to the day was not sustained during the rest of the journey – the road climbed away from the river, forcing me upwards and upwards kilometre after kilometre. It was back to head down, bum in the air and keep pushing. A device I had adopted because I found it useful, was to take my glasses off for these uphill stretches. It meant that I was not discouraged by seeing too far into the distance. This strategy made me more responsive to the pressure required to move the pedals and even though I met what for me were some extreme climbs, I managed to keep going without having to get off the bike and walk. The trick then, however, was to get the spectacles back on when things became easier, so that I could read road signs on the downhill sections. This was a skill only slightly less difficult than that required with the drinking bottle.

Fortunately, the approach to the campsite was downhill for 4 kilometres, and it passed through my mind that there was a possibility that I might stay there, especially if it was a 4-kilometre climb to get out. Strangely enough, I was meditating on this as Damon Hill was leading in a Grand Prix. The camp bar had a television and so I decided to stay and watch as, with only eight laps to go, he was 33 seconds ahead of Villeneuve. The French were getting excited but I watched with English calm, certain that we had another win to celebrate. *Quel dommage!* On the last lap, Hill ran out of petrol and had to settle for second best. His disappointment convinced me that I had to tackle whatever was ahead with pedal power. I had become used to the saddle and although cars sped past at regular intervals I was certain I could make it to the finishing line without having to repeat Hill's walk and push method. It did, however, encourage me to stay put for the night.

I walked into the nearby village for something to do and because it seemed to have attracted a lot of French weekenders. It is an extremely attractive village built on a hill. What makes me do these things I don't know, but I was tempted into walking up to the church at the top of the village – all I needed after a hard ride in the saddle. The door was open and I walked into what was a traditional old church with ornate altar, arched ceiling and side aisles with the Stations of the Cross in the shadowy alcoves. The statue of Our Lady was surrounded by lighted candles. An oldish-looking woman was earnestly praying before her, no doubt for someone ill or someone who had passed away. I could not help but sympathise. The Sacred Heart of Jesus stood to the right of the altar and it was before this that I prayed for the souls of my wife and family. This I promised I would continue to do, knowing that through prayer my wife could find a peaceful resting place and that my children would always turn to Christ, whether in joy or sadness.

The village was small and, judging by my breathing when I had eventually arrived, built on a rather steep hill. It reminded me of that fascinating little town just to the south of Provence, St Jean de Paul. However, it did not have the interest of that attractive little town, and had done little to take up the commercial life that attracts the tourist. The shops were not made to look tempting, lacking the usual paraphernalia for visitors such as holiday mugs or plates decorated with illustrations of the village and its neighbourhood, or postcards appealing enough to send home, but saw their role as tending to the needs of the local villagers. This gave it a charm but did not encourage me to linger too long on its streets.

I made the mistake of eating on the campsite. The guy doing the cooking was miserable and not very communicative. He did not speak English and obviously did not understand my French. The menu contained entrecôte steaks. I could not resist and ordered a steak, cooked medium, with chips and peas. I waited with anticipation, hungry after my meagre rations during the day. What I eventually got was a half-cooked burger. I was too hungry to gainsay it but it was far from enjoyable, even with the French brand of tomato sauce. I was certain that I would find out the next morning what damage has been done. One thing was for sure, I would not be staying for breakfast.

When I arrived back at my tent a couple from Cork had pitched on the next emplacement. I found it relaxing to be able to talk in English and also with such friendly people. We talked about the places we had visited and what our plans were for the future, but only briefly as our conversation was curtailed by thunder, lightning and rain. It was time to head indoors, if that is the right expression for a tent, and hope that all would be well. As it was, the tent withstood the storm, which as far as I could gather next morning had lasted all night and I managed to sleep without any disturbance.

11 August 1997

DAY 11

Alles sur Dordogne – St Cyprien – La Roque-Gageac

I survived the half-cooked beefburgers, I think, but felt a little the worse for wear having had three beers with my Irish neighbours later in the evening. Not being a drinking man I felt a little heady. I know that my wife loved the Irish and our visits to the Emerald Isle and so I felt no guilt enjoying the evening. We had once spent several days in Kerry searching out my grandfather's birthplace and she had been more excited than I was, I think, when we found it. It was an old farmhouse perched on a hill on the outskirts of Listowel. It looked as though it was still inhabited, but there was no sign of anyone to answer the questions we would have liked to have asked. Unfortunately, the parish priest was not helpful either and we could not get to the parish register to research my ancestral background. It may be that we had disturbed his lunch or he saw us as just other visitors to Ireland wasting the time of a busy priest with their facile investigations. Even so, it was wonderful to have photographs of my wife before the door of my grandfather's very beginnings and for me memories of two people that meant such a lot to me.

There had been thunder, lightning and heavy rain during the night but I was lucky to find a break long enough to allow me to put the tent away and get the bike packed. No sooner had I had my morning coffee in the protection of the camp restaurant, than the rains came and my learning experiences started again. It is a fact that when on a bike you cannot dodge raindrops if you are intent on getting from one place to another.

I am told that in Pompeii there is a building in which there are illustrations of over 100 different ways of sexual intercourse. As the guides were on strike on the day I had once intended to visit Pompeii, and as I am not a great experimenter, I will have to rely on second-hand evidence for this. What I do know is that there are many different ways of sitting on the seat of a bike when travelling long distances. The normal way is to sit square-on in relative comfort and pedal. From time to time, it is necessary to make adjustments in order to ease the pressure on different parts of the backside and elsewhere in that region. I found, for instance, that it is possible to ease the pressure by stretching one leg whilst freewheeling and letting the pedal rather than the seat take the strain. To be able to hold that position for a while, especially when going downhill, provided welcome relief. It was also possible to stand on the pedals, putting the weight on both legs and forward through the arms onto the handlebars. This meant that the backside could be lifted off the seat completely. I discovered, however, the most important and frequent movements were that slight shift which is obtained by a quick straightening of one leg or by ceasing to pedal for a moment allowing an adjustment to be made. Such changes in posture have to be made quickly and the skill has to be practised so as to avoid the pain of an uncomfortable re-placement or a dangerous wobble, especially if there was the likelihood of a passing car. I found these movements particularly useful when climbing long hills, and, in view of the distances I had to cover, the practice worth the effort.

Of course, these were normal and good weather tactics for me. I discovered that in the torrential rain there had to be modification. For example, stiffening one leg on the pedal was fine for easing the backside, but meant that my foot and trainer had to be held close to the front mudguard for a longish period. I had thought that the front mudguard was designed to protect the rider by carrying spray over the front wheel and out in front of the bike. I learned that day that this was not always the case. The forward movement of the leg leading to the fixed foot was done without anticipating the backward spray from the front wheel. The inevitable happened; a trainer full of water. Before long, I was squelching along rather like a waterwheel – collecting water if I dwelt too long with stiffened knee on front stops and squirting it out as my legs began to revolve. I had to find another strategy – which meant trying to hold the legs half cocked and thereby keeping the front leg away from the bottom of the mudguard. Once I had learned to do this the situation was eased, though I continued for the rest of the ride with a trainer saturated with water.

I had decided to ride in the rain without glasses – a necessity I had learned when riding along the towpath in Henley. When I coached crews in the rain, I learned that the lack of windscreen wipers or something similar meant that spectacles were pretty useless for coaching, but I quickly learned that as long as I shouted often enough and with confidence something like 'watch the timing' or 'wu-u-u-u-u-uf' in the manner of many other coaches I had observed, nobody was the wiser. In fact oarsmen sometimes came off the water saying that was one of their best outings of the week.

Unfortunately, the decision to adopt the same approach on the roads in France had the effect of reducing my capacity to see much further than the end of my nose and so restricted my ability to see approaching puddles. I have suggested earlier that road engineers give little thought to cyclists, and riding in the rain confirmed this. They have managed to design roads which, in heavy rain, appeared to gather about a metre-wide rivulet of water on the roadside. Sometimes it seemed wider. The result is that the cyclist has to adopt another position, one in which both feet are held high off the pedals with the spray chasing them higher and higher.

Another aspect of cycling in the rain is the increasing significance of other vehicles. The cyclist dare not dodge and weave round puddles; this could put him in danger from some other vehicles, not all of which give the cyclist the wide berth that he appreciates. I tried it a couple of times, but the hooting had me jumping out of my skin. The policy for me had to be to ride as straight a line as I could, accepting the consequences resignedly. It did flash through my mind of course that there was some advantage to be gained as cars and lorries sliced their own route through the eddies of water. Every one that passed at any sort of speed in the sort of rain I was battling with gave me a bath, and if it was a long vehicle a shower and a bath. After the sunny days of the earlier part of my journey, there were aspects of the day that were not proving much fun.

Fortunately, other facets of the journey left me with much to marvel at. Passing beautifully positioned villages such as St-Vincent-de-Cosse and Beynac et Cazenac prepared me, I suppose, for my eventual arrival at the spectacular village of La Roque-Gageac. I was impressed by the traditional narrow streets and well-used houses that had also been well cared for. The honey-coloured stone, reminiscent of Cotswold stone, gave the buildings a charm that clearly attracted tourists, of which there were many despite the rain. La Roque-Gageac was to me special. Many of the buildings date from medieval times, but the village, judging by the historical remains on show, was prehistoric. It is easy to see why it has always attracted inhabitants. Backed by rocky cliffs and protected by the river, it contained all the elements of a village capable of offering protection to its inhabitants. Some of the houses were built into the rock and peered fortress-like over the river.

Nevertheless, the village had not been spared the threat of the Viking longboats which had made their way this far up the river, nor escaped the anxieties of the Hundred Years War and French Wars of Religion, wars which had ravaged France in late medieval and early modern times. The Hundred Years War, intermittently fought from 1337 to 1453 between the English and the French, devastated areas the length of France. English interest was stimulated by the territory it held in the south of France, bequeathed through the marriage into the English royal family of Eleanor of Aquitaine, and the doubtful claims of the English Edward III to the French crown. The wars led to the great battles of Crècy, Agincourt and Poitiers and the renown of the English longbow. It also led to the rise of the redoubtable St Joan of Arc. The eventual removal of English claims to French territory, symbolised by the loss of Calais in 1453, brought the end to wars ruinous to both countries and their inhabitants.

The respite for France that the end of the wars brought lasted only until the impact of the Reformation in France in the sixteenth-century and the Wars of Religion. These outbreaks of rivalry, mainly between Catholics and Huguenots, ostensibly religious, developed into struggles for political pre-eminence. The issues, the cause of much hardship witnessed by the village I had now reached, were only resolved with the politically motivated 'conversion' to Catholicism of Henry IV in 1593.

Little wonder that houses were tightly packed and sought the rock for their protection. Now it was alive with tourists, especially those who took to the water on inflatables of all kinds. This was a village I had never visited before, though I had seen it from a distance as we travelled by car towards Rocamadour. I certainly found it worth a stop and was pleased that I had identified the campsite.

Eventually the rain relented for about an hour, fortunately at the time of my arrival at the campsite, and gave me the opportunity to put my tent up in comparatively dry conditions. Many of the emplacements were fine for a caravan, having good views and access to plenty of electricity and water. It was not surprising to see standing water on most emplacements when I arrived, which gave me fair warning of which places to avoid. I found a relatively dry spot, which I judged to be the best place for my tent. It gave me a proud position overlooking other campers and the feeling perhaps of a general in the field in times past as he overlooked his troops. What I lacked was an aide to do the necessaries for an officer in the field such as make and serve dinner with a good wine. It was not long, therefore, before I headed for the bar. I drank slowly, whiling away my time watching others and hoping that I had made the right choice of site on which to pitch my tent, safe from gathering water. It was difficult to tell. It was only about

2.30 pm and I was sheltering from yet another torrential downpour.

I have never experienced such bad weather in France. I thought to myself that to have only two-and-a-half days out of eleven with sun is not as it should be. I had missed the best of Amboise because of the rain and I had not seen the Dordogne as I remembered it from previous visits for the same reason. I could not believe things would not get better at some point and reflected on this as I dashed back to my tent. I could not avoid, either, reflecting on my squelching trainers.

The rain continued all afternoon and seemed set for the evening. I was amazed at how my small one-man tent was giving me protection from the elements, at least so far. The tent had taken a real battering over the last couple of days but was surviving well. It seemed totally appropriate that the site had a superb swimming pool, and also unsurprising that no one was using it because of the weather.

I decided to spend the rest of the afternoon trying to learn a few French words that might help me on my way but after *mouillé* and *trempé* (soaked) I couldn't think of any others worth learning. By 6.00 pm the rain was more ferocious than ever.

12 August 1997

DAY 12

La Roque-Gageac – Veyrignac – Souillac

A more peaceful day. The morning was overcast but the rain had stopped. Cars and lorries were out in force, but fortunately the roads had dried and they no longer carried the threat they had on the previous day. I had gone 4 kilometres before I realised I was going in the wrong direction! How I managed to make this mistake I did not know but it had its compensations. Passing through Vezac, another pretty village but lacking the stature of La Roque-Gageac, I saw a bank and I was able to get some money from the cash machine. I was running short and needed some to get my breakfast.

The second benefit was that the village also had an agreeable-looking café. Based on my experience of visiting different bars in different places for a bite and a coffee I had come to the conclusion that the patron did not mind customers bringing in their own croissant, or other things to eat whilst having coffee. In this instance, I was more than a little surprised, on asking for a coffee and croissant, when the barman sent me to the *boulangerie* across the road for my own croissant whilst he made the coffee. There were compensations in having to cross the road and join the usual morning queue. A couple of days previously the patron went to the *boulangerie* himself for the croissant and charged me double once he got back and behind his counter. On this occasion I had a rather cheaper breakfast.

Today, I had a lot of time to kill on my own – the one thing I had feared regarding the whole trip, especially as I had taken it to try to help cope with my wife's death and to do something in memory of her that I would always remember. So far I had been OK, because I had travelled good distances, usually beyond my planned route, and spent time at both ends of the day sorting out my equipment, my tent, my emplacements and my meals. In addition, I had found time to make my usual evening notes. Such a routine was helping me see the importance of getting on with life and operating at as normal a level as possible. I had come to the conclusion that this was the only way of coping with such a tragic loss.

Even a year ago, from the day of my wife's funeral, I had resisted the overtures of helpful people, keen to make sure that I was eating properly and that I was not spending my time in lonely grief, and had continued my work. It had not been easy, but attendance at meetings and visiting schools helped me to see that the world carries on despite tragedy and that if I were to remain part of that world I too had to carry on. Within a week of that dreadful occasion I was meeting with fellow professionals, discussing issues of relative importance – for a while they did not seem as important as they once did – and taking on new responsibilities, all of which eased the pain and made living a normal life possible. The responsibility that I had for feeding myself and learning the skills of housekeeping, things that my wife had given me guidance on during the last weeks of her life, were other activities that were intrinsic elements in my coping with my new situation. It was also a blessing to have four children, who seemingly had arranged to take it in turns to ring or visit in the early days to make sure that I was alright. They too were grieving, but perhaps it is helpful to be young at such times.

On this particular afternoon I decided to make a preliminary skirmish with the French rail service. I had become aware that I was entering some mountainous areas and would find some of the climbs beyond me. I had considered turning round at some stage and going back down the Dordogne valley and then taking the south-westerly route through Bordeaux and then across southern

France towards my destination. However, turning round did not really appeal and there were still some sights to see ahead of me. For example, Rocamadour was a place I had visited some years earlier with the family and despite the terrain I was sure I could make it. It would bring back pleasant memories of my wife and children and how solid relationships within the family had been.

On those camping trips we had to pull together to ensure that they were enjoyable. Andrea, having had a background in camping, was expert at knowing what we needed for the trip, how we should pack everything to make the best use of space, which were the best emplacements and in which direction we should face the tent. The rest of us worked together to make sure that all was in order, that the tent was properly pitched and that our belongings were placed in a neat and tidy manner. It was only when these things had been done that we could relax and enjoy what the vicinity had to offer. This is how we worked in rain or sunshine, and these habits were serving me well on this trip.

I was musing on these things as I made my way to the railway station on the first stretch of my journey to enquire about trains. I foresaw myself getting deeper and deeper into the mountains of the Massif Central with a too demanding ride to get out. I wanted to know, therefore, if this was the case and if so how could I get from Rocamadour to Bézier, the latter town seeming to offer a good getting-off point, according to my map, for crossing the Mediterranean strip. Finding the station was a major problem – it was placed on the edge of the town across a canal and down some narrow residential streets. Once there, however, I struck it amazingly lucky. The ticket man spoke good English and took an interest in likely problems – such as getting a bike on and off some of the French trains. I did not fully understand why he was so concerned – I was to learn later – but he went to the extent of working out several routes, all of which meant changes and in one instance a two-day journey. He also proposed riding up a 'hill' sometimes taken by the Tour de France to while away the time at one of the staging points he had identified, but neither of us took it as a serious proposal. After about half an hour of discussion, I went merrily on my way, at least knowing I could get to Bézier by train, eventually.

My next stop was at the local bike shop. For me, going to these places was beginning to feel like going to the dentist – the reason that I was going did not seem so urgent once I got there, I was unsure as to what was going to put things right and oblivious as to knowing what to say when asked what the trouble was. On this occasion, the bike chain had begun to grate, presumably because of the rain, sand and sun it had had to cope with. My best French failed but turning the pedals gave the mechanic the clue. He offered *huile*, a word I understood, but he then offered me a choice, which mesmerised me. He must have seen the glazed look in my eyes and eventually said something which indicated he would put the bike to rights. He took a can of oil and very professionally, while seeming to gabble about the nuts and dryness of the chain, oiled it. It worked beautifully as a result. I promptly decided to buy the tin, hoping that I would begin to look more like a professional when I used it again in a day or two.

Once the bike felt happier it was on to Souillac. The ride was pleasant, though the weather still overcast, but I found myself in an unusual situation. Without realising what I was doing, I managed to enter a small town at the head of a circus. It was as if everyone in the town and the surrounding district was out to welcome the performers. All the show needed was flags flying, drums beating and acrobats a swinging, to add to the trick cyclist, which I seemed to have become, at the head of the parade. I tried to manoeuvre myself out of the parade but only succeeded in getting between the lead car, with its flashing lights and the sign *Grand Convoi*, and the actual convoy. It is just possible that people thought I was the advance guard – they would certainly have found something of interest in me with my baggy shorts and T-shirt, the plastic bags on the back of the bike and the dirty drying-up cloth which had somehow found its way onto the handlebars. There is no doubt that the world is a different place on a bike!

At last I extricated myself and settled by the side of the road until the parade had passed and people had begun to make their way home. I could now remount and continue on my way, which I did without further incident.

Souillac is a town that has the look and feel of English seaside resorts that I remembered from my childhood. It had lots of signs for cheap food, drinks, ice lollies and knick-knacks of all kinds. This rather banal aspect of the town hid some interesting buildings, such as the imposing but, to some extent, neglected church of St-Marie, but I felt that visits to such places were a little outside my remit in view of my journey and the growing pangs of hunger. Instead I looked for somewhere to eat.

I could not see a restaurant of any substance in the parts of the town where I found myself, but felt I should eat well that evening. Having done a tour of the main streets, which revealed pizza and steak and chips to be at the top of the list, I decided to cycle on to the next village in the hope of finding something better. This proved to be my biggest mistake so far. I followed a sign to what purported to be a hotel. Believing I could get a decent meal I followed it. In fact, it led me to a bar on a campsite, and sadly down a steep hill. This I would have to ascend on my return. The menu turned out to be microwaved pizzas, at a more expensive price than those in the town. It was a disaster. The only alleviating aspect was a guy standing at the bar with a Charles Boyer voice. It was a pity there were no women around to be captivated by him. He had the look, the manner and the voice, but no one to entrance with them. All I was thinking was God help me when I have to go back up the hill!

Now that the rain had stopped, the mosquitoes started! Once back at the campsite, I could not believe how many there were and how determined they were to draw blood. They were big enough to allow a study of their long legs, which provided them with a secure purchase for spearing and sucking, at which they were very expert. I had passed a *tabac* earlier in the day, which was selling postcards. The *tabac*, very prominently situated, displayed the human male and female bodies, naked of course, upon which were indicated what purported to be the 14 most sensitive points on a man and a woman. I hesitated to get near enough to identify them closely or stand long enough to absorb the information, as I did not want people to become too suspicious about my motives. I have no doubt that mosquitoes had studied it closely and could have identified more than the 14 sensitive parts of the human frame defined on the postcard. Certainly, they found plenty of mine within ten minutes and left the evidence of their knowledge with me for several days. They included points just above the elbow, the wrist, the soft skin between thumb and forefingers, the back of the knee (particularly painful for the cyclist) and several different places on the calf. After ten minutes of trying to eat some grapes in front of the tent I retired inside, which was, fortunately, largely mosquito proof. Some brave young men had been sitting by their tents in shorts, but it was not long before they were smacking themselves, cursing and then retiring to the bar. The mosquitoes were all over the place, but fortunately a couple of good thumps rid my tent of them for the night.

What is very noticeable about campsites is that camp guardians rarely camp. They certainly do not camp by the side of rivers, for obvious reasons. On most of the sites I stayed, they slept in buildings ranging from châteaux to at least respectable houses and on some occasions away from the site. On only one occasion did I see a guardian sleep in a caravan on site, and he seemed to be a single man who saw his first duty in the morning as tending his flowers.

13 August 1997

DAY 13

Souillac – Martel – Montvalent – Rocamadour

The next morning I emerged from the tent in long trousers, socks and a long-sleeved sweater. I needed them. The mosquitoes were still biting. My protection was mainly successful, and I managed to pack tent and equipment with limited damage. I carried scars, however, from the previous evening and the anti-bite spray, which I had brought with me, was working overtime. Fortunately, it had some effect.

I began to wonder, as I packed the tent, how much of what I had brought was useful.

I had certainly set off with what appeared to be a lot. It is very difficult to estimate one's needs for a month and for the different weather I had already experienced. My thoughts became focused on these at this particular time because I did not know what lay ahead. So far, I had used most things at least once. The map and the Michelin guide had been invaluable, as had the celluloid container on the front handlebars, a suggestion of my daughter-in-law Kirsten. I had discovered that several pairs of underpants were a must, especially as it had proved difficult to wash and dry in wet weather. The three pairs of shorts and three T-shirts also served their purpose. One towel was hardly sufficient, but I doubt if I could have carried more. Sandals were essential, especially as by the tenth day I dare not walk downwind of my trainers. I was just beginning to think that disposable trainers would be the answer, especially when I realised where the smell that followed me from day-to-day was coming from. The sweatshirt and heavy woollen top used more as pillows – something which is essential but impossible to carry when you are mobile – but provided some warmth after one wet day and protection from '*mes amis*' the mosquitoes.

The bicycle tools were essential, though so far I had relied on friendly cycle repair shops, and it had become apparent that chain oil would be needed at some stage. What would have been one of the most useful articles, which, of course, I had not brought, was a piece of cleaning rag. At one of my early stops I managed to borrow an old tea towel off the chef and though I think he thought it was only a lend, it stayed with me throughout my travels, an invaluable article for cleaning the tent, the bike and generally getting rid of wet and dirt. I used all the washing materials such as soap and toothpaste and had to replenish my stocks; the rear and front lamps also came in useful on at least three occasions in early morning mist. The medical equipment was indispensable; so far I had used a plaster, anti-sting ointment, Savlon and Disprin. I had also used nail-cutter and scissors.

Today proved to be a good day to reflect on these things. It was warm and calm and the ride from Souillac to Rocamadour was relatively flat. I headed south from the river and towards the campsite, the Cigales, which I felt sure my wife and I once stayed at with the family. It provided good facilities and comfortable, straightforward tent pegging. So far, this had been one of the better days for weather and for pitching the tent. Blast, those bloody mosquitoes! More anti-sting!

This site was like most I had visited. Campsites seem to come alive when most places would normally go to sleep. During the day they are fairly empty. The environs of the swimming pool might have some activity but most people seem to go off in search of shopping, to visit places of interest, to make a general tour of the area or to head towards their next destination. Come 8.30 pm, when most of the children, if at home, would be ready for bed, campsites are alive with them playing, running between tents or throwing balls in the air or to one another. The water of the swimming pool changes from placid to animated as children splash through it as either the chaser or the chased. It seems that parents hope all the activity will induce sleep once it is time to turn the lights out on the site. At least, this seemed to be the policy on this site. To be honest, I could not blame the parents and certainly hoped that their strategy would work. A restful night would serve me well.

My hopes of an early night were dispelled with the start of bingo. I had seen it advertised and wondered how I would have coped had I been tempted to play. It started around 9.00 pm and campers from different nations had been gathering for several minutes before that. I had come to the conclusion that, tired as I was, I would revise a little French by struggling with the numbers, even if I were not interested in joining them. To my astonishment, the bingo caller used a microphone to call out the numbers and could be heard all over the site. Being forced to listen to *'sept, dix, ou dix-huit'* and many other numbers being called confirmed my earlier doubts, as I struggled to keep pace. An hour and a half of numbers, shouts of 'bingo' and clapping delayed sleep and led me to wondering why I had not followed my original intention of spending the occasional night in a hotel rather than camping. In many respects this would have been a good night to be elsewhere.

I say this, but to be honest, despite the rain, the mosquitoes, the loos and the regular packing and unpacking of the bike, I preferred camping and it seemed the right way to fulfil what I had set out to do. It was Andrea who had introduced me to camping over 30 years ago. Our first trip together was before the children were born. We had hitch-hiked through Holland, Germany, Switzerland and France, enjoying sites situated in places as beautiful as Amsterdam, Heidelberg and Beaune. We made many trips thereafter with the children to places as different as the West coast of Scotland, the Lake District, Norfolk, Brittany, Paris, Bordeaux and Provence. Throughout, we had experienced rain, hot sunshine, mosquitoes, beautiful days and fascinating shared experiences. There were many memories, and I felt it absolutely appropriate to remember her through the exposure to the vagaries of camping that I underwent during a trip she would have understood fully. I know that in her younger days she would also have enjoyed it.

In many respects Rocamadour was the right place to think on these things. It is a superb place. For me, it had much that was reminiscent of Mont St Michel, with the climb to the highest point and the beautiful views. It had no surrounding water, but overlooked valleys rich in vegetation. Rocamadour, nestled in the Lot department of south-west France, is a name familiar to travellers, as well as appreciators of fine dining and rich history. One look at the restaurants, hotels and churches rising magically from the cliffs along the Alzou river and it is no wonder this communal town is one of France's prime getaway locations.

The exquisite natural setting and beautiful buildings have made Rocamadour the target for innumerable tourists over the years, which is not surprising in light of its majestic appearance. It is a place known for religious pilgrimages, a stop for some on the way to Santiago de Compostela, and I sensed something of the spiritual myself as I approached. Rocamadour's churches, especially that associated with St Amadour, a contemporary of Saints Peter and Paul, and the Chapelle Notre Dame with its famous Black Madonna, encouraged contemplation.

The château was the major tourist attraction, seemingly hanging from the cliffs, and it had a variety of ways by which it could be reached, some easier than others. I had remembered from earlier visits that if you chose what could be described as the wrong ones, it meant a steep climb up the Great Staircase with its 233 steps. This route enabled you to investigate the different levels and see what they had to offer, whilst breathing heavily and resting before the next flight of stairs. There was the option of a lift of course, but as far as I remember that meant missing all that was worth seeing, such as the chapels, the sculptures and the caves that offered sanctuary to those who felt threatened at different times in history.

The easier route, and the one I chose, consisted of a fairly gentle incline from the village which provided a pleasant walk to the castle and the ramparts. As I followed the route, I began to remember much of my previous visit, and the sights that the castle had to offer. The advantage of this approach was that the passages to the various lower levels were downward rather than upward, which left sufficient energy to enjoy the sights of the old town. The layout of the town is amazing, planned to make best use of the slopes on which it was built. The streets do not seem to follow a man-made pattern but one dictated by the rock, winding as they did between ancient overhangs and the once protective gates of the town walls. I took my time moving from one level to the next, seeking to absorb what Rocamadour had to offer. For me it was a spiritual sanctuary and one in which I could pray with a piety that was rare for me. Of all the places the family had visited in France, this was the one that I could picture most clearly and the one that the family had found so fascinating. It was unique in what it had to offer.

Once down in the streets again, I was surprised that nobody seemed to be selling anything other than ice cream. This was very different from my previous visits and unusual for a town which entertained so many visitors. Once I had my bearings the usual tourist shops came into view and there is no doubt that sections of the local populace were taking financial advantage of their situation. In winter things would be different and so the summer months were obviously a critical factor in the local economy. No matter, Rocamadour was special for me, as it had been for my wife and family.

I returned to the campsite on a slightly different route to the one by which I had approached the castle, but it was no less charming. Flowers of different types, whether potted and decorating window sills or planted in well-tended gardens, were in full bloom and the overhanging branches of the trees were rich in foliage. My feelings as I approached the campsite were mixed. The sadness remained, as I am sure it always would, but it was no longer outweighing the acceptance of life as it is, and my increasing determination was encouraging me to take strength from my wife's example in her last days and face it full on.

14 August 1997

DAY 14

Rocamadour – Gramat – Béziers – Villeneuve lès Béziers

Today was the day for testing myself on French railways. I enjoyed a pleasant breakfast in Rocamadour and an equally pleasant ride to the station at Gramat. I had been given 12.17 pm as the train time and so there was no hurry, though there was anxiety about how the day might go.

I found Gramat to be very busy; it was market day. Vehicles and people were moving in from all directions, some to deliver, others to sell or buy. The signs for the station were difficult to find and so I stopped to ask. I was in luck. The *mademoiselle* I asked spoke perfect English. She told me that she had lived in Oxford for forty years, though she was French born. As if in shock at hearing someone speak perfect English, the rear wheel of my bike slipped from under me and in front of a line of cars. As luck would have it, their progress was slow because of the congestion and all I got was some not very friendly gesticulations with fingers, hands and arms, accompanied by what sounded like verbal insults. The problem with not knowing the language is that you cannot return the compliment easily. Even the lady from Oxford was unwilling to help me on this one. She was helpful, however, in pointing out where the station was and directing me to it as clearly as if I had been in England. For once, having righted the bike, I made my way with confidence. It did not surprise me that the road led me up yet another hill.

The stationmaster proved to be very helpful once he understood where I intended to go. He worked out a route, showing me with pencil and map, which would take me through Toulouse and to Béziers, getting me there by about 9.00 pm that day. I knew from my maps that there was a campsite in or near Béziers and reckoned that I would still have time to gain entrance for the night if the train was on time. This, therefore, was very good news. I had two hours to wait for my first train and so I left the bike in his care and walked back into Gramat where the market was in full swing. I remained amazed at what people come up with to sell and to buy.

The stalls in France seemed to present a more interesting diet, almost literally meant, than those back home. I had become accustomed to a pattern that was repeated in different parts of the country – clothes, fish, vegetables, household utensils, tools for anything one could imagine and then a range of knick-knacks covering too big a range to describe. There was cooked and uncooked food, most of it clearly produced in the locality, and articles at different stages of completion, encouraging the buyer to try his or her skill at finishing off to their own taste the embroidery or the craftwork. The stalls had taken over almost all the town and seemed to have attracted everyone for miles around. The effect on traffic was horrendous with cars and lorries lined up almost a kilometre back up to the station and a similar distance, I supposed, in the opposite direction. It made one appreciate the bike and, hopefully, the train.

My major shock of the day arrived with the train. The carriage was several feet off the ground and had steps. Now I had foreseen a little difficulty in this quarter and while waiting on the platform had moved some of my belongings to the front handlebars to take weight off the back wheel, making the bike more balanced and easier to lift. I had also spent my time on the platform practising lifting the bike in several different ways, imaging the problems the train was likely to present. I had managed to raise it about two feet without too much difficulty, but I was not prepared for what faced me when the train arrived. It took three of us to lift the bike on. In addition to myself, there was a kindly guy who happened to have the misfortune of getting on the train and into the same wagon as myself, and the stationmaster. With some careful manoeuvring of the bike and personnel we managed to haul the bike upwards and onwards until it was securely inside the wagon. I could not help but hope that I did not leave my friendly station-master with a hernia.

As it happened, my bike was leant against another, which was to prove to be a godsend, because there was no way that the other cyclist could get to his bike until I had managed to move mine. With luck, he would be getting off at the same station as I was. I was hoping that I would have such luck at this point and for the rest of the journey.

French trains travel very quickly, but this one had no air conditioning, or if it had it was not working. As a result, people were steaming and most, including me, could not avoid breaking out in a sweat. The answer seemed to be to sit as still as possible and either read, chat quietly to a neighbouring passenger or sleep. For me, a major problem was that I did not know the route and so I could not afford to close my eyes in case I missed the station at which I had to alight, an interesting word when I reflected on the weight of my bike, to catch my connection. As I had no book to read, neighbour to talk with or the nerve to close my eyes to sleep in fear of missing my station, it meant looking through the window at the passing countryside. This had some advantages in that it meant I saw some interesting sights, at one moment fields of sunflowers and at the next a pretty village bedecked with greens, golds and reds under its gabled roofs and down its narrow streets, sometimes perched on the bank of a stream. Of course there were also the towns of commerce, with their car-locked streets. Unfortunately, the situation robbed me of the sleep I am sure I would have enjoyed, particularly as I was not sure what awaited me at the end of my journey.

At last my station arrived; now for the challenge. As luck would have it, the cycle against which I had leant mine belonged to a cyclist also disembarking. It was clear that he had not estimated the weight of my bike, as he offered to help me to unload. This proved much easier than loading, though it still presented difficulties as the platform was well below the level of the train and there was an inviting gap between the two. I offered to help unload the second cycle, but the cyclist indicated with a gesture of his arm that he could manage. All this was done in silence until he was down on the platform and I had the opportunity to offer a '*merci*'.

The platform was empty and I managed to find a seat near to a pillar against which I could lean the bike. I began to wonder how I was going to load onto my next train, but noticed that the other cyclist was also sitting on the platform. Could it be that he was waiting for the same train? If so, might he offer to help me? To my delight, it became clear that he was travelling in the same direction and he rose as I did as the next train pulled into the station. Again, he offered help and we managed to get my bike into the wagon. In fact, this was to be the case until we reached the last but one station. The poor sod must have been knackered helping to lift my bike on and off. He, too, was carrying a load but was releasing his panniers and taking them with him in the train. This was a ploy I had decided to adopt if I needed to, though I had great concern that the time it would take me to release the untidy load from my bike would see half of my belongings still on the platform and me on the train as it pulled out.

My good luck was holding because at each station I was allowed on to a train earlier than the one indicated by my kindly stationmaster. It meant, in fact, an estimated arrival in Béziers by just before 7.00 pm, a good time for finding and getting established on the campsite. My luck faltered, however, at my last change. The stationmaster allowed me on the Marseilles express train which stopped at Béziers, but only on the condition that I put my bike in the very last carriage of the very long train. There appeared to be no help in sight as I struggled to get the bike on what must have been the highest of the trains I had encountered. Coincidentally, a 'civilian' was passing, saw my difficulty and came to help. By this time, I had managed to raise the front wheel of the bike onto the top step, but in the process had managed to get the front brake lever stuck in my shirt and I was locked between the handlebars and the door. My helper waved as if to say get on the train and he would raise the back of the bike on after me. It was with great difficulty that I eventually squeezed past the handlebars, almost taking my shirt off to get the brake lever free, and got into a position to pull from the front of the bike. The look of shock on my helper's face as he tried to lift the back of the bike was startling. Beads of sweat stood out on his forehead as he struggled to adjust to the weight, but bless his soul he managed and received a well-earned '*merci*'.

Thank God, I thought. I decided to follow the example of the cyclist I had observed earlier in my travels by getting rid of some of the articles I had on the bike, so that it would be lighter and enable me to get it off the train without help. This was going to be essential as I had the rear carriage to myself and it was pretty obvious I was unlikely to receive any sort of support at this last station.

Getting rid of some of the ballast by the time we reached Béziers worked remarkably well. I was able to get off the train successfully, other than for another crack on the shins. I managed to throw my plastic bags and their contents off along with the panniers and then get the bike off before the train began to leave the station. I regarded the exercise as a great success.

I found it very different travelling by public transport than by bike. I could not help but feel that I was being controlled. Trains went at certain times, and I had to be ready to board; I had to have tickets that were inspected at regular intervals, and I was dependent on the goodwill of others as I sought a seat or thought about opening a window. When I had watched people queuing in cars in the towns I had passed through, following great lorries and looking impatient, or seen buses pass by with sweating passengers, I could not help but enjoy the thought of the bike. What the train journey proved was that the bike gave a freedom which could not be replicated. I had the advantage of fresh air, the scent of the countryside, time to observe what I passed in whatever detail I wished, and, most of all, I could get on and off when it suited me, park wherever I wanted, walk or ride and still get to my planned destination, eventually.

15 August 1997

DAY 15

Villeneuve-lès-Béziers – Vias – Sète –

Palavas-les Flots – St Laurent d'Aiguze

Today was the Feast of Our Lady's Assumption. I had to find a way to get to Mass but was in danger of missing out as it was at 10.00 am in the village just outside Bézier at which I had eventually stopped. It was here that I had found a campsite, but one that I could only describe as having rudimentary facilities. The 10.00 am Mass was too late for me as I had a fair distance to cover and by that time I would be well on my way. I was worried that the best I could do was say I had tried. Then, as luck would have it, I arrived in Palavas-les-Flots just in time for an 11 o'clock Mass. I had seen the church from a distance and cut off down a side road to investigate the possibilities. I had begun to get the right sort of feeling as I saw people walking in the same direction and more and more parked cars.

The church was a modern construction reached by climbing steps outside. I managed to find a post to which I could attach my bike and lean it against a wall. I then left it on trust, believing that my belongings and bike would be there in an hour's time when I returned to them after Mass.

It is easy to say that the atmosphere in a French Mass is different to that in an English Mass. It is far more difficult to say why. The ritual is exactly the same, and the English prayers that I was reciting more or less in unison with the congregation fit more or less with the timing of the French prayers. The sermon in this church was slightly longer than in my experience in England, but that could also be a difference from church to church in England, depending on the priest. But it contained more gesticulations. I could not understand much of what was being said, which was a pity, but the French seemed to show about the same level of interest as a congregation in England. Some appeared intent, others were alert from time to time and others seemed to be dreaming of the post-Mass lunch, which would no doubt replicate the famous Sunday lunch enjoyed by many French families.

The overall involvement of the people was about the same as in England. They read the lessons and the bidding prayers and brought forward the gifts for sacrifice. The mixture of reserved and closely involved people within the congregation and the apparent average age, which one might kindly describe as middle, was about the same. What was special was the presence of the cantor for the singing, a rare occurrence in England. It struck me as being very French. Also, there appeared to be less discipline within the congregation, with people being more prepared to move about or chatter to one another from time to time than was my experience in England. It was this informality, I think, which was the key to the different feel I had for the Mass.

In addition, the way the French made use of the exceptional also made things a little unusual. On this occasion, for instance, a visitor, who had been introduced at the beginning of Mass as a good accordion player by what appeared to be one of his relatives, was invited to play. Sitting on the altar before the priest started the prayers for Mass, he helped to create that essential prayerful atmosphere by giving a moving rending of Gounod's 'Ave Maria'. At the end of Mass he reappeared to send the congregation home almost with tapping feet as he played an Ukrainian dance. I assumed that this reflected his country of origin. No matter, he did it with style and panache, entertained the congregation, most of which stayed, listened and gave him resounding applause as his performance came to an end. The whole experience was one in which I could readily share and wondered why we did not make more of such talents in our own churches, where the pattern rarely changes.

The day was very different to any of the previous days. I had made a relatively long train journey the previous day and was now in new territory, the South of France. What I had hoped was the case, the roads were mainly flat and I now had a rhythm which enabled me to sustain a good pace for longish periods. What I had feared also was the case. It was like pedalling into a wall of heat. It was indeed hot on the Mediterranean coast. What breeze there was came from the sea. There was a little, very noticeable when riding into it, but it was hot and did little or nothing to cool a sweating rider. As my mouth dried and I realised that my attempts to create moisture with the use of my tongue were doomed, taking on liquid became central to my thinking. Thank goodness that I had practised the art of drinking while riding. Now I was an expert, able to bend, take hold of my water bottle, throw my head back and drink or pour water over my face to provide the fluid so important to completing my journey. The knack I had developed of replacing the bottle without a moment's anxiety demonstrated the progress I had made towards becoming a real cyclist, but my skills had not yet extended to being able to ride without hands or handle downhill gradients without being constantly on the brakes.

With it being a Feast day, many shops were closed. I decided, therefore, to deviate from my planned route to find the supermarket that had been well advertised on the latter part of my ride. Unknown to me supermarkets were closing at 1.00 pm, the time I arrived outside one, short of water and gasping for a drink. I also thought I might get something there for lunch. The entrance door was closed, which I thought was unusual, but someone came out of the exit with shopping so I nipped inside. I found the aisles empty of people but couldn't find where the water was stored or make my mind up as to what to get for lunch, a circumstance which was not entirely new for me. Eventually I found the water and then came across the shelf containing yogurt, which I thought would contribute in some way to a healthy lunch.

It was at this stage that I became aware that the only people moving up and down the aisles were in uniform. Once collared I realised they had been looking for me; whether they thought me a crook searching for a hiding place in preparation for a big robbery that night or an idiot who was breaking the rules, I never discovered, because I didn't understand a word they were saying, and they were doing no better with me. They shepherded me and my bottle of water to the cash desk where I met more trouble from a frosty, ill-tempered cashier who had just cashed up. The water I had bought and the additional yogurt cost only three francs and the smallest note I had was a 100 francs. God! I was lucky to escape with my skin. The cashier had to unlock her till and presumably do another cash reconciliation because of some idiot who had managed to find his way into the shop after closing time. I was unceremoniously led to the exit, pleased not to be able to translate what was being said behind me. Having looked shifty and uncomfortable inside, once outside I became somewhat nonchalant, taking time to fill my water bottle from the bottle I had just bought, drinking off the excess in sight of my 'captors'. I then mounted and rode away as though nothing unusual had happened.

The search for a supermarket had led me from my planned route. As a result, I managed to get lost several times, but in a sense that only added to the interest of the day. I found myself in places which I would never have visited, but which were fascinating. To get lost on the newly created dock area at Palavas revealed an incredibly well-planned, integrated development. On another day I would have found interesting shops to look round, different activities in progress and the general excitement associated with a busy and lively place. The town harboured a great variety of boats and gave the impression of being built solely for that purpose. The area was well enclosed and I could find no natural exit. The only way I managed to escape the area was to follow another cyclist, who was oblivious to my presence. He led me round jetties, walked ahead of me up and down ramps, and eventually led me back to the main road. What I had seen of boutiques, small hotels, restaurants and all the paraphernalia of the sailing life was worth the anxiety.

Equally fascinating was the ride along the shore of the Mediterranean. I was glad that I was too old to be interested in sun, sea and sand, because the number of people squeezed into all available spaces made me wonder what enjoyment the Riviera now offered the innocent holidaymaker. It was clear that the sun and beach worshipper had a routine to follow. The first job was to find a car park, an art in itself. Once this was accomplished a scout had to make for the beach to find a space large enough to contain the family. The scout was followed by those who had to carry their sun brollies, towels, ice boxes, sun lotions, balls, wind protectors and whatever else they needed to claim a piece of beach which had been marked out as their territory. What seemed kilometre after kilometre of sand was covered by couples and families who had obviously gone through this process. At one pedestrian crossing – road markings largely ignored by French motorists – I was almost upended by the advancing brolly of what appeared to be a legion on the march. I suspect they were about to stake out an area into which interlopers would fear to tread.

There is no way of winning with roads. With the ups and downs of the north and centre of France behind me, I mistakenly looked to enjoy the flatness of the 'Région de la Petite Camargue'. The Camargue has a beauty that is not replicated anywhere else in France. Famous for its birds, its white horses and black bulls, it also has unique varieties of flora such as tamarisk and narcissi. This was an area that I had travelled with the family on our camping holidays. It was a place that we rarely stopped in or even looked for a campsite, having been warned of its heat and the likelihood of strong winds, the enemies of campers. I had also seen the Tour de France cross this area as one of the flat sections and heard commentators talk about its debilitating effects. I was not surprised to find the long, flat roads stretching as far as the eye could see or to find that they offered little respite from the burning sun. On occasions the road became as disheartening as the roads that had towered above me on previous days. Today I did 100 kilometres in order to clear the Camargue. I found it physically easier, but psychologically equally demanding as the hills that I had encountered earlier on my journey.

As I moved away from the sea and further inland I saw Montpellier rising in the distance. I had heard that this was a beautiful city and worth visiting and it was a place that I had never been before. This tempted me to make a diversion from my been route, but I resisted the temptation and headed for the campsite in which I had planned to spend the night.

16 August 1997

DAY 16

St Laurent d'Aigouze – Vauvert – St Gilles –
Beaucaire – Avignon

Today it dawned on me that I had become more or less acclimatised to France and the hotter weather. I still drank a lot, I needed fluid to replace the perspiration I suppose, but for the last couple of days, despite the heat, my tongue felt that it was the right size for my mouth and I could eat a croissant in relative comfort. There was also a marked difference in the number of times I felt I had to have water. I took all these signs to be good.

My itinerary had been carefully planned before I set off but it had been blown to pieces by the distances I had been able to cover daily. I was now in Avignon, seven days before my planned date of arrival. The flatter roads from Bézier to Avignon had given me more control over the timing and speed of my travel and so my pace was not being dictated by the need to climb or descend hills. It gave me more opportunity to think.

The French take the Feast of Our Lady's Assumption more seriously than the British. It is a public holiday and a day of obligatory Mass. Judging by the many placards I had passed on my way through France, there are also many different kinds of festivities organised to celebrate the day. It set me to wondering, on this relatively quiet cycling day, on the meaning of life.

I believe in God and I believe that the Roman Catholic Church is the one true Church. This position is based on my belief in the life, death and resurrection of Christ. I had been taught these things as a child and I have read about, and reflected on them since. The last of these has always been the fundamental basis of my faith, though I know some Christians would have a different concept of the Resurrection to mine. For me, it still means resurrection of soul and body, but thinking of my wife's body in her grave did not help me understand the mystery. Inevitably, such a belief creates problems and raises all the doubts that the non-believer, as I understand it, has as certainties. I had sat at peace in churches with a lot of French people, worshipped the same God, no doubt petitioned for similar things and through Mass followed the same liturgy. Yet I could hardly communicate with them, knew none of them and, oddly enough, did not feel the need to know any of them. Yet I believed we were all destined for an after-life, body and soul. That was not to say that we would all end up in the same place, for despite the softening of teaching within the Church in recent years about Heaven and Hell I still believed that they existed, though in what form I was not clear. They were not realities to me in the same way as the Resurrection, because they were not of this world. The Resurrection was in some respects the outcome of a worldly life, sacrificed for love; a life that had all the feelings and emotions that we as mere mortals know of and to some extent understand, but which had that extra dimension that belonged only to God. In a similar way I saw Heaven and Hell as a human does and was incapable of seeing them in the way that both the Old and the New Testaments sought to portray, despite what I had read in the Catechism. For me they represented human actions and emotions and the good or harm they could cause. They were, in a significant way, the outcome of being human.

Cycling along at a steady pace in peaceful weather I was encouraged to continue my thoughts on the meaning of life and death. Another aspect that had always intrigued me was how we relate to one another after death. Would we need to communicate with one another and if so how would we do it? Would there be any interdependence between us and would we have sufficient independence of thought and action to be able to make decisions as to how we would exercise that interdependence? Would our relationships with the host of relatives and friends who had preceded us or were to follow, and for whom we had prayed for so many years, be the same or different to those whom we had never known before death? What of my wife and would we ever meet again? And what of those who, according to the message of Christ, did not deserve to make it to paradise? If I had friends and relatives amongst those and I had been lucky enough to make it, how could I be happy in their absence? In this world, the death and absence of a loved one leaves a deep pain which hardly fits into the concept of heavenly happiness. How could it be different if I knew I would never see such a dear one ever again? What does all this say about a just God? At least there is hope and belief in this life that through prayer those who have already died will meet with us again at some stage in the future. How could I not wrestle with these thoughts if I was to find some solace in my wife's death?

It was thoughts such as these that occupied my mind as I pedalled towards Avignon and tried to fit them into the simple interpretation that I have of the after-life. It was particularly pertinent to me because of the reason for my journey, the recent death of my dear wife. If some of these questions could not be resolved, how could I rid myself of the pain that I had felt during the past months? Would I ever know what had happened to her? Knowing her as I did, living with her and sharing the same faith, these were thoughts I turned over in my mind. From those early days of our courtship, when she had told me that she was about to be received into the Church, until the day she died, she had been resolute in her faith. Together we had brought up our four children with that faith and trusted that our example would serve them well in the years to come.

I have always felt that the greater the understanding one had developed of God and of his meaning for us in this life the better prepared we would be for meeting with Him in the next. In the same way that we moved closer to and related better to those we loved on earth, so it was with our relationship with God. The more we understood Him, spent time with Him in prayer and sought to follow His teaching in our actions and thoughts, the more likely we were to be prepared to meet with Him. As far as I understood it, the Saints had a deep understanding of God's meaning for us, and they had not necessarily gained this through great learning or through consistently living the life that Christ would have wanted them to. It was their love for Him and others that led them to sacrifice and to that deep understanding that affected their lives on earth, and helped them prepare for their meeting with God better than the great majority of us could. This is why they hold such a special place. So, in my simple theology, we shall only be able to experience and enjoy God's wonders at a level commensurate with that understanding we have of Him, and in this sense it enables us to inhabit one of the many 'houses' Jesus talked about when referring to Heaven.

None of this pondering on my journey to Avignon resolved any of the questions I had posed myself, but it did help to confirm my belief that the more I lived a life in line with Christ's teaching, the more likely I was to meet with God. Not surprisingly, this helped to ease the pain of loss I was experiencing and strengthened my belief that in death my wife was benefiting from the many blessings she had bestowed on others during her life on earth.

Of course, these theological musings cannot last long on a camping holiday. They are superseded quickly by more practical things, such as trying to follow route signs through a major city such as Avignon with the only guidance in the Michelin being to head north to the Ile of something. The saving grace is often the river. Follow on the left or on the right and at least you have a bearing; that is, so long as you are on the correct side of the river when you pass the campsite. Fortunately, I was.

100

The campsite was well positioned. It was within walking distance of the town and spacious. I found an emplacement without trouble and had plenty of room to set out my belongings and put up the tent. I had arrived early enough to give me time to make a foray into the town, just to get a feel for the place and see what I might do on the next day. This pleasant sojourn in Avignon was brutally interrupted by one of those storms in which the lightning and thunder seem to coincide. The storm caught me in the middle of a bridge between the shelter of the town and the campsite. I got so wet because of the heaviness of the rain that by the time I reached the end of the bridge there was little point in sheltering under the only leaf that seemed to protrude far enough to give any cover. Water was trickling down the back of my neck, into my shorts and flattening my T-shirt to my chest.

The real crunch was that I had taken my family's advice to wash clothes from time to time. Today was one of those times and I had emptied my panniers and washed everything. My clothes were hanging on a piece of string tied between my tent and a nearby tree. The string was no doubt trying to cope with the increasing weight of every heavy spot of rain while I was seeking some form of protection on the bridge.

At last I decided to make a run for it and sped through the teeming rain to the campsite. Wet as I was, I felt I should take a shower and so avoid the possibility of catching cold. The string, though bowed, was still in place and so I grabbed a towel and headed for the shower. What joy – wet through, no dry clothes and a tent which gave you hardly any space to have a cat, never mind to swing it. It took half an hour in the shower, a day in which I tried to dry myself with a soggy towel off the line, and a patient wait in wet shorts for another 20 minutes while watching the rain gradually coming to stop, before I could get back to the tent. Once inside I found dry pyjamas and a dry sleeping bag, enough to give me the opportunity for sleep. For once, I believed that the tent was secure and well enough pitched to cope with the rain. My good fortune was demonstrated next morning when I saw couples who had either tents of poor quality or who had failed to secure them properly for the night, sleeping outside their sodden tents, clearly having tried to find somewhere dry to sleep during the night. Happy camping!

17 August 1997

DAY 17

Avignon

Today was a rest day. At 6.45 am the noisiest refuse lorry ever crashed its way round the site, devouring all the rubbish sacks, of which there seemed to be many; so much for a quiet morning. Even so, 7.30 was not a bad hour to rise in view of the other days when I had risen earlier.

I had left all my wet clothing out on the line but rightly had no hope of it drying overnight. I made my way for my morning shower, after which I dried myself again with the soggy towel. At least the sun was rising and, as it was already getting much warmer than I was used to in England, things were likely to be dry by the end of the morning. I breakfasted at the campsite, but my clothes were still wet by the time I had finished. As I wanted to get to Mass in Avignon my solution was to take a T-shirt, still wet, and carry it over my arm, as open as I could, in the hope that it would dry.

Being at the northern end of the Camargue I must have looked an interesting site retracing my steps over the bridge to Avignon, now in bright sunlight. The shirt was largely red, and hanging over my arm as it was, I must have looked like a bullfighter. From time to time, a deft flick to turn different parts of the shirt to the sun gave me the feeling of the matador and when halfway across the bridge a headwind encouraged me to hold the shirt out in front of me. I could visualise the bull, horns down, on the charge coming at me, with me on my toes, shirt held in bullfighter position and ready to dance out of the way. What a way to enter Avignon! Of course, it was all make-believe, but reality returned when I decided I had to put the wet shirt on as the quickest way of drying it.

Avignon is a fascinating place – full of history and still carrying magnificent signs of its past. It once sought to establish itself as the home of the Papacy, and for some time during the fourteenth-century it successfully did this. Pope Clement V made it his residence as he fled from political turmoil in Rome and from 1309 until 1377 it remained the seat of the popes. Thereafter came the bitter struggle with Rome and the great schism which continued into the fifteenth century when claims to be the papal seat were eventually renounced and Rome once more became the home of the Papacy. But the Palace of the Popes remains, to my mind a baleful reminder. Room after room of bare walls failed to parade the opulence that they once contained. The descriptions of papal affluence and the pampering the Pope received left one with a deep despondency. Descriptions of the help with which he was provided to dress, to dine and to entertain, especially on what were described as 'state occasions' such as the visit of Emperor Charles IV, seemed to leave little room for that spiritual leadership expected of one in such a revered position. Fortunately, only the beautifully laid-out gardens of the palace remain a reminder of former aspirations and glories. I could not help hoping that the Vatican of today offered a better model.

Leaving the Palace, I wandered through the streets and squares, most of which, but especially La Place de l'Horloge, are given over to cafés and shops. The town seemed alive with business, even on this Sunday morning. People were sitting out already, having their breakfast of coffee and croissants, talking, laughing and, in the main, enjoying their Sunday morning. A few, more sombre, sat alone reading the morning newspapers, legs crossed and, as often as not, cigarette at the ready. The bridge, or to be accurate, half of the bridge, Pont St Bénézet, upon which people danced according to the song 'Sur le Pont d'Avignon' that I used to sing in French lessons at school, remains as the symbol of Avignon to me and I suspect many other English holiday-makers who get the chance to visit the city. Not surprisingly tourists still flock to it and pay whatever the cost to walk what remains of it.

I approached the square down La Rue de la République, a busy thoroughfare, passed through it and made my way to Notre-Dame-des-Doms for Mass. The church was full, with a congregation that was clearly of mixed nationality. The commitment of Catholics on holiday to their Sunday Mass is evidence that secularism has not yet conquered all. The priest was welcoming and the worshippers reacted with committed and clear responses. I had no difficulty in such an atmosphere in praying for those dear to me and believing that God would listen with compassion.

I followed Mass with another enjoyable walk around the town. I decided to join the coffee brigade in the main square and observe, without any particular purpose, those who passed by. Nobody seemed in a hurry as they meandered from one place of interest to another, zigzagging between others on the same mission. After a while I decided to do the same and to enjoy the relaxation.

I had a simple lunch in town. It consisted of little more than pasta and coffee. I sat observing passers-by with interest, distinguishing between the tourists and the locals as best I could. Somehow the English stood out with their shorts, ankle socks and sandals, the traditional Englishman's dress abroad and one that often amused the local population, who rarely wore socks. The English were also identified by their white or red legs and necks, though I suspect that this colouring applied to most visitors from northern Europe. I could smile contentedly, having gathered a French-like tan on my way through France. Because of the rainy days I could not help feel that rain has as much impact on the skin in its own way and produces that weather-beaten look that those of us abroad are often seeking.

On my return to the campsite I found the environs of my tent alive with *moustiques*, as they had come out to feed during the late afternoon. I had also noticed them in the early morning, but had had little time to experience their effect because of my attempts to deal with my wet clothes and prepare myself for Mass. Now, they

105

were out in force and I could see why Avignon had become famous for dancing. One had to step from one foot to the other in the hope of disturbing them and avoiding their bites. These *moustiques* were different to those in the Dordogne – not as big or obviously vicious, but there were more of them and they bit almost imperceptibly. It was their cumulative efforts that eventually began to wear me down. Hiding in the tent or in the bar gave me some respite through the evening, but they were more than a little challenging. There is no doubt that on the morning I left I had little interest in how I packed the tent and my belongings or how I loaded the bike – speed was of the essence as I became more and more frustrated and aggravated. I could not get rid of the blighters and my dancing must have been a sight to see. It was a pity I was not on the bridge.

Which brings me to considering two characters who were clearly campsite regulars. I have written earlier about the different individuals and groups that inhabit campsites during the summer season. These two seemed to be special. One, a poor man's Johnny Hallyday – or at least that is what I think he saw himself as – dressed in jeans and cotton shirt and wearing large dark sunglasses drifted around the site, sometimes with a knapsack slung from his shoulder, but always with an air of untidiness. He seemed unconcerned about what was going on around him or what others might think of him. He had a sway from the hips which I thought was a throw-back to the 1960s and was the sort of fellow one would meet at the bar, drinking beer at 8.30 am. When not drinking or swaying, he sat by his tent, which was half hidden by bushes, listening to his particular brand of music. The T-shirt that hung from his line read 'Sorry, no auditions'.

The other character seemed to be constantly in search of an audition. He was a rotund little man who carried his stomach low and held it up with his belt. He too was half hidden by bushes in an area rarely frequented by other campers, but I knew where he was because of the tinkling sounds emanating from his guitar. He never seemed to play a recognisable tune, and it was never loud enough to be disturbing, so I assumed it was a modern form of practising, as he prepared for his big night. What was for sure, on the move he looked like a musician in search of a band because whenever he emerged from the environs of his tent he had his guitar case strapped to his back. And he walked with briskness, as if to suggest he had an important engagement to fulfil. He walked through the campsite and disappeared into town on two or three occasions whilst I was watching. I saw him in Avignon several times on my day's excursion, always with the guitar case seemingly at the ready on his back, but never with a guitar in hands in performance mode.

I draw attention to these two characters to further demonstrate the complexity in the make-up of the camping fraternity. There are those like me who use sites as a means of getting from one place to another, staying one and at most two nights; there are those who use them as a base from which they can do other things and may stay up to a week; and there are those for whom the site is their holiday centre and the proliferation of facilities such as swimming pools, games rooms and restaurants reflects the camp organisers' response to this. And then there are what I would call the camp 'groupies'. My two characters fitted this body. It was difficult to know when they came or when they were likely to go – they seemed to have become fixtures. They knew the campsite workers, the best deals and seemed perfectly at home adjusting their life to a relatively cheap form of accommodation that gave them the opportunity to be whoever they wished to be. Their sort of camping seemed to be a culture associated with the 'flower people' of the 1960s and one which some had yet to grow out of.

18 August 1997

DAY 18

Avignon – Châteauneuf du Pape – Orange –
Bourg St Andeol

As I indicated earlier the morning was unlikely to start well. The *moustiques* were waiting for their breakfast and I provided it. Henceforth, I shall wear tracksuit bottoms and a long-sleeved top at feeding times, an approach I had forgotten since the Dordogne. I had failed to restock with any of the appropriate protection, such as insect repellents, ointment or spray, and somehow could not keep the blighters off me. A swish of a towel or a smack with a hand did nothing to deter the squadrons that seemed to have learned their skills during the blitz in the Second World War and so the only solution was to run for it.

I made a hasty exit from the campsite but failed to take time to check my bearings properly. Therefore, I had a period of anxiety as I left because I was not sure that the route I had taken would get me off the Ile de la Barthelasse the largest 'unspoiled' (the French description) island in France. However, I need not have worried as I had made the right decisions for once and found the road I needed.

It was the start of a pleasant ride along the Rhône. I breakfasted in Châteauneuf du Pape at what I thought was a reasonable price, except the bread seemed old and a well-worn baguette has major limitations; it is similar to eating a sponge. This surprised me because my last visit to this town had been with my wife and we had thoroughly enjoyed it. It was with the extra interest, therefore, that I had approached it. We had booked into a rather splendid rustic-looking hotel overlooking the main square on that occasion. Andrea had always enjoyed involvement with other people and to be able to look down from the window and see so many scurrying here and there, carrying boxes of wine, fruit and vegetables gave her great pleasure. What would I have given to have back one of those seemingly distant days? I would certainly have held on to it for all I was worth, loving her excitement and sense of adventure as we viewed a spectacle we had so often talked about when discussing what we should do in France. On that occasion we were a middle-aged couple unaccompanied by our children, and free to do as we wished during the summer months.

I have always been impressed with the bottles in which most of the wines from this area arrive in English supermarkets. It always appeared that the coat of arms of some noble family had been cut into the bottle to announce the high-quality wine drunk only by aristocrats. If this was the case then I was the exception, being no more than a hard-working coal-miner's son, but this did not prevent me from being impressed by the bottles and enjoying the wine. With this in mind, Andrea and I had taken the opportunity to visit one of the prestigious *caves* where we were guided through the process of wine making. One could not help but be impressed and the odd glass at each stop made the experience even more enjoyable. Not surprisingly, when the hustle came at journey's end we felt obliged to spend far more than we could afford to take away a case of the cellar's best. So different to the experiences we had had in Epernay when savouring the delights of champagne at the end of a journey through the cellars of Dom Pérignon. There, there had been no hustle and visitors were left to wander to look at the different illustrations depicting the making of Dom Pérignon. Those guiding us treated us at the end of the visit as they had done throughout, with respect. If we wanted to buy we could, if not, then the fact that we had shown enough interest to be there seemed to be sufficient for them.

On this occasion, my visit to Châteauneuf was a fleeting one, a visit designed to give me the opportunity to reminisce and get what strength I could from the memories as I began to prepare for the future.

Now my journey took me towards Orange, an extremely busy gateway to central France. How I had managed to manoeuvre myself across the river and onto a busy thoroughfare I am not sure, though a later check with the map showed me that my diversion to Châteauneuf du Pape was probably the reason. I was looking forward to visiting Orange, though I did not intend to stop. My interest was in its history as an important base in the Romanisation of that part of France and I was hoping to see something that remained a reminder of those distant days. I knew that there was a Roman theatre, which I was unlikely to see. But there was also the Triumphal Arch, a sight of which was a possibility as it was likely to be in the vicinity of the main road, as was the case with the arches in London, Paris and Bucharest. What I had not bargained for was the traffic. Here I again became involved with *un convoi exceptionel*, though on this occasion it was more the result of a long tailback of cars and lorries, rather than a circus, patiently making their way through the busy thoroughfares of the town. I had the advantage of being on the bike, which enabled me to weave in and out of the traffic, but my loading had been so rushed and untidy that I could not avoid the odd skirmish with a driver as I scraped past his car. I had to be more cautious with the big lorries because I was never sure that the drivers could see me creeping down between them and the pavement, despite their specially designed wing mirrors. I made decent progress, however, and my anticipation was fulfilled when I saw the majestic arch built by the Romans. It lacked nothing of the grandeur I had expected.

My planned camp for the night was Pont Saint Esprit, which was described as very attractive and quiet in the guide book. Heading for it was a mistake. The road took me over the river and then back over 7 kilometres towards Orange to a site hidden in trees and on what looked an ill-kept farm. It did not appear in any way appealing and so I decided not to tempt fate and to turn in search of a better-looking site. I pushed back beyond my 7 kilometres to the next site indicated in the guide book, which was at Bourg St Andeol in the vicinity of the Ardèche. By this time I was out of drinking water, an outcome of my mastering the art of imbibing while still on the bike, and was beginning to struggle because I had already covered a good distance and some of it had been at a slow pace because of the terrain.

For the first time on the journey I was beginning to feel the tiredness that I had been awaiting since my landing in France. I had managed without major difficulty but now the ache in the legs and the arms, so long anticipated, began to materialise. Worse was the throbbing in the hands, caused by the vibration of the front wheel on the many different road surfaces. I had been advised to wear cycling gloves or mittens but not about the juddering that the hands bore throughout a long ride. It was a new experience for me and not a pleasant one. I had begun to experience shaking hands at journey's end each day and I began to wonder if the sensation was to be permanent.

Notwithstanding, without thinking too much about the consequences, I was now faced with a deviation that I had not bargained for. The ever-increasing number of hills seemed to extend the length of the ride even further beyond my expectations and beyond what I had prepared for. Fortunately, I managed to get liquid at a slot machine, relax tired legs, and consider what next. The rest sustained me until I reached the campsite and the big bottle of water I had begun to dream about.

The town in which the site was situated seemed to have closed down for Monday. Only the odd shop was open. Fortunately, I found a *pâtisserie, boulangerie* and a bar. This allowed me to stock up for breakfast and buy something that I could prepare for tea. It also enabled me to visit the bar for a drink. I found the clientèle of the bar interesting, as it reminded me of something I had noticed earlier with regard towards attitudes to race. For the second time on my journey I found myself in a bar which was frequented entirely, from the dress, especially the topi and overall appearance, by what I took to be Muslims or Hindus. The waiters were, I guessed, Muslim and the drinkers were Muslim. I have no idea what they were drinking as I understood that most Muslims do not drink alcohol. The drinkers in this bar reminded me of what I had experienced sometime previously at St Giles, where it was only when I had begun my drink that I realised everybody who entered appeared to be Muslim and male. I must admit that nobody seemed bothered about my presence and I was not made to feel unwelcome, but it was noticeable that other French passed by without giving any hint of wanting a drink.

According to a recent survey there are four million Muslims among a population of forty plus million in France. I was not sure what messages I should draw from these two statistics though I found it interesting enough to muse on the overall relationship between Muslim and non-Muslim, the opportunities offered to Muslims for work, their general treatment in society and how the school system coped with any difficulties that might occur because of the differences in faith, religious practice and dress. I knew that in England there were confrontations from time to time in those towns to which large numbers of immigrants had gravitated, which sometimes spilled over into riots, but I knew too little of France to get beyond asking myself the same sort of questions I might have asked in England. As it was, I had seen lots of examples of mixed-race couples and mixed-race families on my travels through France, and on the campsites the youngsters, no matter their colour, seemed to play well together.

As I left the bar and walked down the street to the campsite I was reminded of another feature of the France through which I was travelling. Everybody seemed to smoke, young and old, male and female. I supposed there was a limiting age for youngsters, but it was difficult to establish it as I observed those who were smoking in the towns and villages through which I had passed. Time and again, the only purchase I had observed in the different shops at which I had stopped was a packet of cigarettes, whether it be early morning or late evening. I could almost guarantee that when a woman went into her handbag or a man into his pocket it was for a cigarette and if they were carrying anything in their hands it was usually a packet of cigarettes. A puff, a cough and another puff seemed the order of the day. What this did for the French health system I did not know, but I had first-hand experience of what it did for individuals. I had seen my father waste away with lung cancer, exacerbated by his years down the mines, from smoking and the lack of good medical care in the days when doctors in our village were skilled at diagnosing without inspection, always assuming that chest infections and early death were inevitable for miners. I had also seen my wife's mother and father, both heavy smokers, die from lung cancer. If anyone needed a warning, I had plenty of examples. What was always fascinating about those who should have heeded the danger signs was their belief that it would not happen to them.

19 August 1997

DAY 19

Bourg St Andeol – Le Teil – Le Pouzin –
St Laurent du Pape

I have not discussed the relationship of the French and their dogs before because I have been trying to work out whether those I observed saw their dogs or children as more important. Certainly, they seemed to treat them the same. Dogs accompanied their owners into restaurants and enjoyed some of the pickings from the expensive meals, had a couture fit for a lady, and were allowed to roam, seemingly to do what they wanted and being chastised only rarely – or at least that is what it seemed to me. On the morning of my departure I had a large Labrador puppy helping me to pack up the tent, its paws all over, putting the fabric of the tent at risk of damage. Nobody called it or seemed to be concerned. It eventually tired, leaving me in peace, but then lolloped across to a woman and child. The child was terrified of the dog, started screaming and the woman had difficulty shooing the dog away. Nobody chased it or called it. Within seconds it happily half jumped, half ran across in playful mode to a child of about two who was unsteady on her feet, knocked her over and started pushing her with its nose. This stirred the owner who seemed to have been aware of the dog's frolicking all along and he eventually came to her aid. The owners then proceeded to chastise an older child, presumably for not looking after the toddler or the dog, or both. Whatever, the dog went bouncing on its way seemingly having a great time.

Wherever I went, I found owners and dogs. Clipped dogs, shaggy dogs, dutiful dogs, happy dogs; dogs with chins on restaurant tables, dogs under the restaurant table, quiet dogs, barking dogs; prim dogs, shifty dogs; dogs' heads hanging out of car windows, dogs sitting between driver and passenger as if guiding the way; dogs on laps, dogs in shopping baskets; big dogs, little dogs; dogs on leads, dogs roaming; dogs sniffing and dogs being sniffed, full of it; dogs on leads with nose and tail in the air, dogs scratching and worrying; wherever you looked, dogs. I even passed a dog cemetery and a boutique for dogs. Though the last do exist in England, they are not so evident as they seemed to me as I journeyed through France.

The French attachment to dogs seemed unwavering as it was also to some of their other pets, for example, the monkey I had come across earlier in my travels. It was not surprising, therefore, that I passed at one busy crossroads a man protesting on animal rights. What struck me was his appearance, which made me wonder whether or not he had ever thought about his need for human rights. He was either very sunburned or dirty, and I suspected the latter, as there was no obvious means of sanitation within miles. His van, which stood just off the road, was in a parlous state. It was dirty on the outside and bore the marks of confrontations with other vehicles. I suspected that the inside would be little better. It may have been his sleeping quarters for all I knew though it was not one of those rather expensive motor vans that I was used to seeing on the campsites. It was well worn and looked a fixture. No matter its appearance. The protester's flag was flying high at the rear and his message, *Non a Vivisection*, was clearly spelled out in what I took to be symbolic black paint. It struck me that people with a cause are prepared to go to great lengths to share it with others.

It is true that my own family had had dogs. The children loved them and my wife took the major responsibility for looking after them. In fact, she had wanted a dog from the early days of our marriage. Although I had been used to dogs about the house since my childhood days – I remember a fox terrier and a Yorkshire terrier – I was not desperately keen to have a four-legged friend at that time. I had managed to put off the inevitable with excuses about having young children, about needing time to look after one and the cost of feeding a dog. It seems that my wife had somehow forgotten that she had a dog at home, Jacquot, when I was wooing her. It was a black poodle, a very popular breed at that time. It seemed to know what I was about and, filled with jealousy, it nipped the back of my leg as soon as it set eyes on me. It persisted in trying to do so every time I visited. Fortunately, the family eventually recognised the problem and called it to heel before further damage could be done. As a result, he lost the battle over his young mistress. That experience was mirrored later in life when we lived on a smallholding across from Ilkley Moor. For some reason, farmers' sheepdogs had a similar tendency every time they saw me.

Anyway, my wife's disappointment about not having a dog was obvious and so the day came when, passing a dog rescue centre some miles from home, impulsively I went in and chose one. The manager of the centre was delighted to have a customer and showed me a variety of dogs from which to choose. I eventually settled on Sam, as he was to be called later. Without thinking of any likely consequences I sat Sam in the passenger seat next to me. Since then I have had nightmares as to what the outcome of such a move could have been. Fortunately, he remained impassive, observing the passing scenery as we made our way home. He was clearly delighted to be out and with friends again. He was received joyously by the children when we reached home, by my wife disbelievingly, and was soon one of the family, responding well to the loving care he received. He was a mix of boxer and Labrador.

Sam was incredibly gentle with the children and with others. But he would fight any other dog that came within his sights. This caused me embarrassment on more than one occasion. The classic was on a camping holiday to Scotland when he sat quietly by the tent until a small poodle came sniffing around. Sam took off at speed and the poodle even quicker, and the pair of them dashed in and out of tents causing all sorts of mayhem. My first reaction was to laugh at the sight, but the consternation growing in neighbouring tents brought me to my senses and I set about catching him. As I sought to retrieve him, I came in for the sort of abuse that leads you either to be a fighting man or to pack your tent as early as possible and head for the hills. As it happens I am not much of a fighting man, despite being brought up in a mining village. There I had learned there were three choices – fight, bluff or get out quickly. I had used all three in different circumstances, sometimes making the mistake of thinking, to my cost, that smaller guys were easy meat. On this occasion, I decided to take the third course of action. Fortunately, the hills were our next destination! Early next morning we quietly packed the tent and our belongings and slipped away from our emplacement and headed for our next campsite.

As for our second dog, Jason, he was much fussier and less of a fighter. My main recollection of him was the shock on the face of our visiting parish priest as Jason took off from the centre of the room and landed on his lap, licking his face. Such was my experience with dogs, which explained, perhaps, why I was so interested in the French approach.

My journey took me to a campsite that was Dutch-owned and very well run. Most of the clientèle were also Dutch and appeared to have taken over this little part of France, if only for the summer. Most of the signs on the site were in Dutch and the first language tried on me was Dutch. If I had not pedalled every mile from Avignon, I could have believed I had been picked up and set down in Holland. It was a good site though, because everybody was anxious to keep it clean, tidy and in good condition.

The journey from Avignon had been a particularly pleasant one. The road was mainly flat; it followed the Rhône and from time to time gave magnificent views of the Rhône valley. The road I had taken was to the west of the river and some distance from the motorway, which passed mainly on the other side. This was a great blessing, because it meant some peace and quiet and time to reflect on the countryside. Some of the villages and their ruined castles were quintessentially French. For somebody who had been brought up in school at a time when wall maps of the world were mainly red, when Britain was always at the centre and when everything that was best, we were told, was British, it still staggered me to see history of a different, but in some senses more majestic, type unfold as I cycled through France. Cathedrals, churches and châteaux span the ages from the Roman conquest to modern times in almost every part of the country I visited and much of what we have in England seems to be largely based on its influence.

The only reason for this can be that few people who taught me or talked to me about historical Europe in my younger days had either not spent time abroad, or had been unfortunate enough to see Europe as a war-strewn parody of what it was at its best. Even in primary school, where one of my teachers had recently returned from war, there was little but British history taught. The marvels of the Empire were passed on to us, the next generation, who, I suppose were expected to imbibe, believe and preserve.

I also remember colleagues from my time in the army who had also served and could only describe, in the main, the ruined cities that they passed through. Few people of this generation or of an age to be able to influence me had had the pleasure of the Grand Tour, which earlier, and wealthier, generations had enjoyed. It was only when I was much older and reading for a history degree that I began to understand a slightly different story of the British Empire and to be able to put those earlier lessons into some sort of perspective. Observing what the Rhône Valley had to offer, I meditated on these things. I reflected on the prayers that had been said for the soldiers, both living and dead, and on whatever side they fought, and the candles lit for generations of young British men who had died prematurely in different parts of the world, often for reasons they did not know or understand.

Here there were reminders of battles long past and of castles that offered shelter to villagers threatened by invaders, some from foreign lands but others from their own country seeking to extend their power and influence. The common ground for safety seemed to be the highest hill or nearest rock. It was here that fortresses of defence were set as challenges to invaders. One striking example, in the village Rochemaure, was of a deserted castle that reached to the sky seemingly growing out of the very rock upon which it stood.

20 August 1997

DAY 20

St Laurent du Pape

This was a good campsite. I had continued to make good time and was closing in on my destination and so it seemed sensible to take the opportunity for another rest day. The weather was good, and the surrounding countryside looked very appealing. Perhaps I could take the opportunity to rest a weary backside and walk.

There was no coffee, or what most English would call coffee, on the campsite! I could buy bread or croissant, cake or Orangina, but no coffee. I was staying for another day and so had to forage – that is walk the 15 minutes into the village to pay 17 francs for a *café au lait.* I then went to a nearby shop to buy something to eat. Although it was early morning there was a sizeable queue, mainly of women, searching for fresh bread for breakfast. This seemed to be the custom in France, a practice that I had seen several times before, not only on this trip but those the family had made previously. Two sticks of bread and several croissants seemed the norm. My order was more simple, but said in what I thought to be impeccable French: *Un croissant and une tarte aux pommes.* The shop assistant's amazed look when I asked for these in single quantities seemed designed to make me ask for more. But I only needed one and so, despite her checking the number twice more, that is what I stuck to. This was by far less than the average French shopper, many of whom seemed to be stocking up for a siege. I bought water and consumed all to complete breakfast.

I then thought about what to do – a walk was the only possibility because, looking at the saddle of the bike, I did not want to ride and neither did I want to sit about the campsite all day.

It seemed to make sense to replenish my water supplies and buy something for lunch. Without a touch of embarrassment I went back into the *patisserie* and with a '*bonjour encore*' asked for another one croissant and one tarte aux pommes. It was the shop assistant's look of resignation which made my day.

I walked out of the valley high into the mountains; they felt like mountains but they may only have been hills. It was a pleasant walk in many ways, though the steepness of some of the hills and the heat of the sun brought perspiration. I stopped from time to time to look across the hills that stretched for kilometre after kilometre, virgin territory that I felt sure man had never trodden before. But closer inspection proved me wrong. At the highest point that I could see, someone had built a fortification, now in ruins, and there were several farms, at some distance from each other, spread amongst the hills. Each seemed to have its hayfields, sometimes steeply banked, surrounding it, the crop freshly cut. It reminded me much of parts of my native Yorkshire, where I used to get out into the woods and fields, which provided the opportunity to observe the birds and look for their nests, seek to identify the different trees, and enjoy drinking from the cool sparkling streams. It was also possible to walk within a few yards of the farmhouses that surrounded the village.

In my childhood days there had been none of the infilling with modern buildings that has since taken place. It was not unusual for us to spend our autumn half-term holidays earning sixpence a day picking potatoes or weekends helping at a local farm. I have often thought how lucky we were to enjoy on the one hand the camaraderie bred in an industrial village and on the other the open country just five minutes' walk away. On this day, as I reached what seemed to be a plateau high above my campsite, the memories of my childhood captured my thoughts and reminded me of friends whom I had not seen for many years. I could not help wondering whether they would still remember me and how many

I would remember if I ever returned to my village. Most had gone to work in the mines and no doubt would bear the scars.

Here, from a distance, the fields looked like well-tended lawns, cared for by farmers who, like farmers everywhere, loved their land. As I progressed on my walk I realised that increasingly there were fences, and notices with the word *privée* or signs saying *reservée de chasseurs*. In this part of France there did not appear to be much, if any land, which seemed to be left unclaimed. It was beautifully tended and, although all was quiet on this hot, sticky afternoon, reflected the hard work of the farmers. A mixture of stock farming and crop growing seemed the common approach. Animals grazed peacefully, or sheltered from the hot sun under trees, the cows listlessly swishing their tails.

I could not help my thoughts drifting from this idyllic site back to my native island and to begin to wonder about the miles of apparently unclaimed land in Scotland that I had often seen. When Andrea first took me on what was a memorable hike through the mountains she knew so well, I remember being astounded by the amount of land that had seemed untouched. I saw no notices on that hike and felt a million miles from anywhere. So hot had been the day that we had crossed land to swim in a smallish loch, oblivious as to whether we were trespassing or not. I used to enjoy our trips to Scotland, occasionally an alternative to the Lake District or France for a camping holiday. The coast around Mallaig and Arisaig, long before television and good radio reception had reached it, provided an ideal spot for campers, despite the rain. To be reminded of such happiness and the recollection of the children, happy to be with their parents, as I wandered through the French countryside made this journey worthwhile. Indeed, Andrea was in her element, organising the cooking, making sure that the clothes were clean and dry, organising and re-organising the tent depending on which way the wind was blowing, and constantly reminding me to take my boots off before I walked in.

Eventually I headed back to my tent, covering the same ground that I had walked over earlier. I was seeing the view from a different perspective, but it was equally beautiful and still capable of bringing back memories.

On the campsite I had a rocky patch, much like the one I had encountered earlier on my journey. I was back to wondering how to get my pegs into the ground. I worked on the principle that if I could get about an eighth of an inch purchase I was in business, and anything better than that would give me some hope if a slight breeze sprung up. If anything other than a slight breeze blew up, I had visions of the flysheet heading for the Ardèche gorge.

Of course, the real campers were well prepared for rocky ground and brought out the heavy armaments; solid pegs which looked as though they could pierce a tank and hammers with solid heavy metal heads. The arrival of a party of Dutch in several mini vans and with several tents epitomised the efficiency which my approach lacked. Their section of the site became what I imagined a scene from *Dante's Inferno* should look like with the banging of metal on metal, flying sparks and perspiration everywhere. The rock had no chance as the pegs ripped through it, sending bits flying in different directions. Before long a laager of well drilled tents, reminiscent of those of the Boer Trekkers of South Africa designed to protect the settlers from the indigenous population, emerged as order out of chaos. The owners were quickly into their stride, with calor gas burners, pots and pans, and seemingly enough food for an army. They settled as one big family, passing round what looked like appetising food, tools with which to eat it and glasses of red wine. They took their time over the meal, chattering and laughing and clearly enjoying the experience of camping. No doubt they were regulars, as were many Dutch, who seemed to find the trip from Holland, through Belgium and into France, much to their taste, especially as they had no Channel or similar to cross.

For my part I had metal pegs which hardly pierced the ground but which were strong enough to hurt my toes with disturbing regularity as I stubbed my foot against them as I moved around the tent during the evening and the following morning. Even so, my pegs did the job for which they were designed, helped by the calmness that embraced the site, and the tent stayed put through-out the night. The advantage I thought I might have over my Dutch camper friends was that when the time came for packing away, my pegs would come out with ease. As I thought, the next morning I was able to take out the pegs, pack the tent and be on my way in no time at all. I did not stay long enough to find out what happened to my neighbours and I never learned what piece of machinery would be needed to remove the rock-crunching pegs. But wait, I am ahead of myself.

Encouraged by the style in which others had been eating on the campsite the previous evening and comparing it with the measly fare I had bought for myself, I decided to go out on the evening of my rest day and eat in style for once. I had spent part of the day looking at various eating places just out of interest, but also to check on prices. They varied greatly, from snack-style eating houses to good-quality restaurants. The prices did too, but I felt that the time was ripe for a meal of substance. I decided on a restaurant. The one I chose was well-presented and the menu attractive. The price was less so, as I dipped into my pocket to find an amount – the equivalent of £20 – which was more than I thought I should be paying as a fully fledged camper. No matter; it was excellent French cooking with an appetising starter, a rare steak, and a delicious dessert, rounded off with a tasty carafe of house wine; a meal which had my lips smacking for many a kilometre afterwards. I had entered with style and confidence, despite my attire, which identified me as a camper to anyone who cared to notice; ruffled shirt, well-worn shorts, socks and trainers. At least I was clean and as far as I knew did not smell of anything other than soap, having had a shower just before I left the campsite.

The visit to the restaurant also gave me a further opportunity to observe a French family out for the evening. On this occasion there were no dogs or monkeys, just a family consisting of mum, dad and several children. They were clearly enjoying their visit and their meal. There was constant noise, some argument (almost inevitable with children), some laughter and the sort of passable manners that gave the table what might be described as a lively appearance, with paper, utensils and glasses all over the place. I didn't know whether anybody minded or not that the table was left in such a state. Certainly nobody seemed to. Order was only restored when it came to paying the bill and then it became clear who had overall responsibility. The waiter took the money from 'Pap', as the children called their father, and whatever tip was left, returned change with the mandatory sweet, and the family departed, noise unabated. Once they had left the waiter went about his business with obvious resignation, clearing the rubbish and the wherewithal that had been used for eating. Within minutes, the table was back to its pristine best, looking as if nobody had been there and ready for the next customer.

Having enjoyed my dinner and what had become an evening's entertainment I paid my bill, leaving a reasonable tip. I left my table in what I thought was decent order, said '*bonne nuit*' and headed back to the campsite, hoping for a good night's rest.

21 August 1997

DAY 21

St Laurent du Pape – St Peray – Tournon sur Rhône –
St Vallier – Andance – Albon

I had said a mental *au revoir* to the Dutch and their rock crushers, I did not know how to say it in their language, as I headed north towards Viesine. Again, the ride was pleasant, with the smell of flowers and fruit, richer scents that you never seem to get when in the car. Rows of peaches, apples, pears and the vines of the Rhône made the journey something special. I was now riding easily and with confidence, having developed some of the skills that had been beyond me on earlier days. To take the bottle, drink and then replace it was now a simple activity, and the balancing of the bike had become almost an art. I took the customary coffee and croissant, how French I had become, at the next village, and later in the morning refreshed myself with a beer. My next challenge was to find myself some lunch.

One of the things I had noticed throughout the trip was the confusion the arrival of a single person caused to campsites, restaurants and shops. Campsite prices were usually geared to emplacements with *deux personnes* and an extra charge for additional children or adults. The arrival of one person with *vélo* invariably led to some complication – either I was charged as for tent and two, or some adjustment was made, on what scale I never discovered, and for a price which appeared nowhere in the literature. As a result all seemed to be left to chance and the generosity of the site manager. The beauty of the single camper of course is

126

that he makes limited use of facilities and with a small tent can be squeezed into a small space, leaving room for another tent, sometimes holding a couple of campers.

Restaurants were equally confused. Even in the best that I visited, all the tables were set for two or more. The arrival of a single diner invariably resulted in an apprehensive response, a discussion between two or more waiters and then the re-setting of a table, usually one set for two and often in an inconspicuous place. In the best establishments the removal of the spare chair and eating implements followed naturally. In the less salubrious places it could result in being plonked at the end of a table set for other diners. Alternatively a seat might be offered at a table not yet set but which was hastily prepared, so as not to spoil the regimentation of the restaurant's preparation for dinner.

This lunchtime was different. The restaurant displayed itself on the prominent sign, which seemed to challenge one to stop, as 'Hotel/Restaurant' and stood at a busy crossroads. It turned out to be primarily a transport café, essentially for lorry drivers but into which odd individuals like me strayed. Tables were all set in fours, no tablecloths but paper serviettes and glasses, knife, fork and spoon. Whilst I was weighing up my options, as I stood in the entrance, and considered carrying on my way, *madame* pointed unceremoniously to the buffet bar and rattled something at me in French, in which the word *entrée* appeared. My dithering ceased in front of her steady gaze and I made my way nervously to the bar. Having helped myself to what was a decent spread, I was about to choose a table near the window when *madame* attracted my attention and pointed a firm finger to an empty seat at a table of four, already occupied by three brawny lorry drivers with tattooed arms and clothes looking as though they had missed the washer and ironing board. There was no arguing. I meekly joined the three others who I assume had found their places in the same way. We made the usual courtesies, which I could now do with a nonchalant '*bonjour*' and then shared the basket of bread, the water and the carafe of wine as if we were old chums. Thankfully, nobody spoke a word throughout the meal and so I could chomp away without embarrassment. This was not true of all the tables of course. At some there was great convivial chatter, but obviously among drivers and their mates and those groups who were regular visitors.

Madame went through her routine several times with other would-be diners as though she was a sergeant-major of the old style, and not even the toughest-looking lorry driver seemed willing to challenge her. This continued until all the seats were filled. Once we had finished our starters, we were given a choice of beef or some kind of *poulet*. I went with the flow, nodding when asked by my table mates what I wanted next and I think chose wisely because we were presented with a communal dish from which we helped ourselves. If I had made a personal choice and gone for beef, I think I would have been the first slice. As it was, chicken arrived.

I have never seen chicken so big. The wing and breast was the size of a small turkey. Anyway, we all helped ourselves without a word, eating plenty and leaving plenty, adding vegetables from our dish as we felt appropriate. The main course was followed by a plate of *fromage blanc* or *varié*. We all had the same, sharing the bunch of grapes which also arrived. With a cup of coffee, sugared from the shared bowl, the lot came to 68 francs. For about an hour, I had been a French lorry driver, but other than '*oui*', '*merci*', or '*au revoir*', I said no more than if I had been sitting at a table on my own.

I received the usual welcome at the campsite –

'*Une personne, un vélo, ah. Suivez-moi.*'

It was a good site and had the now common *piscine*. I asked for the price and the guardian didn't deign to give me one. This left me wondering whether she thought it not worth the trouble making out a bill, or if she needed an hour or two to make a calculation. Tomorrow will tell.

I find the different shapes and sizes of people incredible. A swimming pool on a campsite is the place to study this phenomenon. In a normal pool, especially the enclosed ones we usually have in England, the range is less obvious, because, youngsters apart, those who frequent them tend to be swimmers or keep-fit people, or those wishing to show off their bodies. Overweight swimmers, women especially, seem to be able to cloak it in some way, occasionally by a one-piece swimsuit, and have the sense not to wear those flimsy two-piece 'swimsuits' worn at the poolside by those on holiday. Most spend more time in the water, less preening on the side, and so hide to a large extent their flabbiness. On a campsite, because it is a holiday and most are visitors from northern Europe, the purpose of a pool is different. It is a place to sit around, to relax and to get a tan. It is a place where everybody feels the urge to join in: thin people, well-proportioned people, tall and short people, old, young and middle-aged people, but seemingly most of all, fat people.

My thoughts turned to this because I was attracted by the army of ants which paraded backwards and forwards across the patio. One was lugging a dead wasp, sometimes going straight, sometimes in a circle as if to get its bearings. But I wondered – are there many different shapes of ants which come out of the same anthill or nest as human beings out of a tent or caravan? To the naked eye they all look the same size as well as colour. For the life of me, I could not visualise a really fat ant bearing a load often twice its size disappearing through the hole or crack from which its family was emerging.

The question of colour also came to mind. The ants that I could see were all the same shade of black, though I have also seen red ones elsewhere. The campsite swimmers are all shades – the white body, bright pink going to red, a mixture of red and white depending on which part of the sun had touched, as many shades of brown as could be imagined and the occasional black. In these ways, the camp *piscine* reflects 'holiday man'.

22 August 1997

DAY 22

Albon

Another rest day. I am nearing my destination at a faster rate than intended and I am slowing my progress by increasing the number of nights on campsites if they are pleasant. This one is, but there is little around it within walking distance to fill a day and so it is back on the bike to find places of interest. I suspect the main attraction is in the neighbouring hills but I cannot be tempted to cycle into those. I stay on the main, lowland, routes as a result, following the Rhône north and then turning to follow it south. There are some splendid views of the river, but the villages and towns it washes seem to contain little of real interest. Certainly, as far as I could judge, they do not hold the pleasures of the lower Rhône where the gabled houses, pots full of flowers in bloom and the churches reminded me that I was in France.

However, I am now finding cycling enjoyable and have developed the skills that can afford me the time to ponder on my surroundings and enable me to look around without fear of falling off. There is no doubt that cycling without my normal load offered a different perspective on my trip and made me wonder why I had not taken advantage of occasionally staying overnight in bed and breakfast accommodation or a small hotel. No doubt such a mode of travel would have introduced me to another aspect of French life, but being a Yorkshireman by birth I had thought of the expense, compared the expected costs, and decided on camping. I had not regretted it and despite the rain and the *moustiques* had enjoyed an experience which brought back so many fond memories of earlier days with my wife and family.

What I did learn on this day's outing was that steady cycling over time keeps the mind and body active. Despite my appearance, which still reflected more closely a ragamuffin than a true cyclist, though my skin was now tanned, I had travelled far enough to feel confident in any group of real cyclists. I could sustain a steady pace for a reasonable distance, turn in the saddle to talk to passers-by, sing without discomfort and even bend to take a drink of water without falling off. I felt good and a sharpness in my thinking prepared me for different eventualities. I had conquered the fear of the passing of great lorries that either seemed to suck you under their wheels or blow you off the road, and of English drivers who came so close that they seemed to be unaware of the cyclist, especially this one, a technique more unthinking than the much more careful French. I now had no difficulty in picking up the various scents of summer flowers and fruits, and seeing the latter growing into full ripeness. I was even beginning to distinguish between different birds and had the skill to slow or quicken in response to their actions in order to follow their movements more closely. This day's cycling helped me to realise how I was coming to terms with the tragedy of my wife's death and my changed circumstances. I knew that there was still much grieving to do but the journey was easing the heartache, especially as it had a purpose beyond human materialism.

There are parts of the day which are different for the lone traveller. In my experience, they tend to be in the hour or so before and after evening meals. This is particularly so as a cycling camper, because your tent is too small and hot to retire to and you have no books to read, even if you can find a chair to sit in; books are too heavy to carry with the rest of the bulk the bike needs to bear. There are times when you could find other companions with whom to sit and talk about whatever people talk about – the events of the day, the people in the next tent, the French and their dogs, planning the future, philosophising; such gossiping was, in my experience, the stuff of companionship. Its occurrence was rare, however, and there was little to do but watch, think and imagine how different things might be.

On this evening, all I had to do was look at the ants parading across the ground in front of the tent and occasionally across various parts of my body. I was amazed at their work rate. They were always on the move, searching in all directions. It was fascinating to see them dragging a crumb or a leaf twice their own size back towards the hole in the ground from which they had emerged. On some occasions, they struggled past other ants going in the opposite direction, and on others, another ant would stop to give help. How they knew, from the level at which they were working, what direction to take, especially when having to detour to avoid a slight tuft or a stone, intrigued me. So did their efforts to get a too large crumb into the hole. In the main they ignored what was going on around them and displayed the sort of determination and concentration that I envied and admired.

It was inevitable that observing the ants led me to thinking about humans and how we responded to different circumstances. It was obvious to me and everyone else, I suspected, that we behaved in much more diverse ways, seeking a range of outcomes and generally developing different ways of achieving them. Consequently, we were normally less regimented than the ants, and only in particular circumstances do we operate in similar ways. On the whole, however, I am of the opinion that humans tend to find ways of deviating from the norm and presenting their own personalities. Whether this means we were more or less productive or more or less efficient I did not resolve that evening and probably never will.

I was aware that when I had been regimented in military uniform during my national service I had come to realise how important regimentation was. As a raw teenager, I had entered the barracks for Guards training with some apprehension and my concerns were not dispelled as I was marched down the drive at a quick pace by a more experienced trainee to what was to become my home for the next 12 weeks. By the time we reached the stark brick buildings I was jogging to keep pace and panting as a result. I had to get used to early rising, the spit and polish of boots, the 'Brassoing' of buttons, and the morning bed inspection which could result in having to scamper down two floors to retrieve washing and shaving kit along with other personal belongings if the trained soldier had emptied the contents of what the inspecting officer regarded as an untidy bed through the window. On at least one occasion, the whole bed had disappeared through the window. In addition, I had to learn to march, to salute, and to jump when told to do so, as well as polish to gleaming brightness coal buckets that were to be immediately filled with coal. Obeying orders became second nature, the response unthinking and unquestioning.

There was no doubt that such training, along with all the other joys reserved for us by our superiors, led to regimentation, a regimentation breeding an *esprit de corps* essential, I had come to the conclusion, for a decent fighting unit and one in which one could rely on comrades. Without that confidence nothing could be achieved. It was something of this *esprit de corps* that I had observed in the ants and which led me to admire them for their efforts on behalf of their 'family'.

My observation was interrupted by thoughts of my need for food. I have eaten a fair number of campsite meals during this trip – I suspect that few cyclists of my type have room to bring their own cooking equipment, and even fewer have enough energy for cooking once the bike has been unloaded, the tent pitched and preparations made for the night. The meals I had eaten on campsites had varied greatly in content, quality and price. Generally, they were not as appetising as the tired cyclist, or more importantly I, would like. When I had the opportunity, I went to nearby restaurants, recognising that these also varied in quality, but hoping they had, as most seemed to have, a trained chef. Having a son, John, who was a highly trained chef and once a senior chef at one of the top London hotels gave me a little insight into what to expect in good quality, and campsites were not the places to find it.

On the campsite it often seemed that the cooking was done by a member of the family who had followed a do-it-yourself course, or a local who probably had made *commis trois*, about the lowest echelon in the more decent hotel kitchens in England. It was not unusual for the cook also to be the waiter – that is unless all he or she did was shout from the counter that the steak and chips are ready for '*numéro douze*'. The most regular dishes that I had come across on campsites were related to *frites*, eaten there or taken back to the tent, some form of beefburger, or pizza, occasionally with a choice of topping.

Some of the higher-starred sites went a little upmarket, not with the quality of food, sadly, but by providing tablecloths. On very rare occasions a three-course menu was offered, with a menu and cooking of similar quality to the beefburger and chips, but priced a little higher. All I could think was that there must be thousands of half-trained and untrained cooks operating in France in the holiday season, all contributing to France's great gourmet tradition. In general, the caravanners have it right – buy at the supermarket and cook your own. This evening, I was eating at the campsite, looking forward, as hungry cyclists do, to enjoying *salade verte*, as it was spelled on the menu, lasagne and chips, and a dessert I could not interpret, all for 68 francs. '*Bon appétit!*'

23 August 1997

DAY 23

Albon – Sablon – Condrieu – Vienne –
Meyrieu les Etangs

Today is wedding day. After a desultory ride across flat, open terrain I hit upon a wedding. The churchyard was full of cars with balloons and streamers and the church so packed that it was almost impossible to get in. In fact, the invited guests seem to file in and file out to take a peek at any arriving family, the bridesmaids and perhaps to look for air in a way I have never seen at an English wedding. Dress was a mixture of formal and informal. I counted about four suits, one topped with a black French beret, several jackets, all of the loose-fitting type – once upon a time we would have called them too big – a number of ties and little boys with bow ties. Trousers were of varying kinds from designer to jeans.

It was the women who stole the show, many in chic dresses clearly bought for the day and some looking very fetching in the way they sexily glided up and down the aisle. The to-ing and fro-ing in and out of church went on for over half an hour and then the photographers appeared and took over. Encouraging family and friends into the churchyard they created little scenarios of mums, dads and children, girlfriends and boyfriends in pairs and groups, families and friends all photographed in different postures and under different trees. Then flowers appeared on the church steps and I had the expectancy of the appearance of bride and groom. But then the first hat appeared, either the bride's or groom's mum, on the arm of a suit, and then a second likewise.

They stood to be photographed and then disappeared into the crowd, a practice very dissimilar to that which I am used to in England, where mum seems to hold pride of place for quite a while, being photographed with every relative that can be found. Then came what appeared to be the preparations for bride and groom. The latter, or at least I assume the latter in this case, must be a footballer or *pétanque* player, as from nowhere appeared a team of red jerseys, embarrassed-looking young men with footballs, who dutifully lined the steps under the direction of the photographer. They made an arch in readiness for the arrival of the to-be-wed couple. Facing them stood the *pétanque* team, each with a gold *boule*, held out as if in readiness for play. The players were dressed in all styles and shades of clothing. The guard of honour waited, the bride and groom appeared – she in white, splendidly attired, he in a dark suit – and the photographer clicked.

All this was different to my experience in England, where it was common for the groom and best man to be in church long before the bride and where it was regarded as the bride's privilege to arrive late rather than early. At my own wedding, my dear wife and I had followed the tradition as, with a Papal blessing, we committed ourselves to join together until death did us part. What joy, and now what sadness. I wished better luck on those to be married today.

I decided to re-enter the church, as much out of curiosity to see what sort of service was used to consecrate a couple in marriage as to see the behaviour of the congregation. In essence, the service was the same as the one I had experienced, but there was much more fidgeting and photographing among those gathered to witness the joining of the young couple in wedlock than I could remember in an English wedding. Where the English presented an air of piety throughout the whole ceremony, the French seemed to provide one of joviality.

After the ceremony the bride and groom kissed to the clapping of those present and the clicking of cameras. As the happy couple progressed down the aisle the clapping continued and what I took to be shouts of congratulations rang out from different parts of the church. As they entered the sunlight they were greeted with more cheering and the arch of footballs and *boules*. The smartness of bride and groom was thrown into high relief by the rather raggle-taggle appearance of the odd mixture of sportsmen on the steps of the church. Here, more photographs were taken. So many people were involved that it was difficult for me to distinguish the mothers and fathers of the happy couple, but I assumed that they were in several of the groups that were assembled to be photographed for posterity. I know that to this day, my own children have photographs on display that bring back so many memories of my own happiest day.

Once outside, and clear of the photographers, the jollifications started in earnest. Everyone piled into cars and the hooting started as they drove to the hotel in which I guessed was to be enjoyed the wedding feast. It was every bit of 100 metres from the church door. The cacophony of noise coming from cars was supplemented with the church bells. Believe it or not, horns were still hooting at 7.15 the next morning when I began to have breakfast.

Today had also given me the opportunity to visit a town I had always passed by, Vienne. Roman monuments are scattered liberally around the town and most are easily accessible. They include the restored Temple d'Auguste and the Théâtre de Cybèle. Of particular interest to me was the Cathédrale St-Maurice, dedicated to one of the first Roman soldier martyrs, a church I had read much about. I understood it to be the most famous of such buildings in Vienne and I was not disappointed. The impressive nave and beautiful stained-glass windows were worthy of a man who had died for his faith on the banks of the Rhône towards the end of the third century.

After all the excitement of the wedding and the pleasure of Vienne I moved on to the nearby campsite. I was met by two 'guardians', the oldest of which must have been four. They watched my every move – where I put the bike, what I took off it and my conversation with the receptionist. They had angelic faces and when given the opportunity spoke to me in words I did not understand – other than for one, 'Orangina'. I was gasping with thirst and had bought a can of Orangina. As I stood by the bike preparing to drink it, their eyes grew bigger and bigger and they began to communicate more urgently in the word they seemed to know I understood, 'Orangina, Orangina'. The outcome was a shared can of 'Orangina *frais*', two smiling faces and one unquenched thirst. I saw one of the boys several times subsequently, but he didn't seem to show the same interest in what I was doing.

The campsite was interesting in that it overlooked a lake, the name of which I never learned, but which was clearly a French playground. Hundreds, it seemed, of French were sitting around on the sun-scorched grass picnicking, conversing in the way the French converse and keeping an eye, or so I hoped, on their children paddling or swimming in the lake. The blue sky touched the hills on the far side of the lake and the blue waters lapped against their base. It made a splendid scene and one which rekindled some of the best days I had spent with the family in the Lake District. Such situations never failed to bring back memories, even though it was often of joy pierced with blades of sorrow.

I had a good spot on the site, giving me a good view of those around me and those enjoying life further afield. Before the evening was out, I was joined by English neighbours. It was a very pleasant interlude to talk in a language I understood and to find such interesting people nearby. They were very experienced holiday cyclists, having done the Munich–Milan run, several other areas of France and parts of Switzerland. They were into hydraulic brakes and dynamo lights, things which cyclists like me hardly understood or could only dream about. The husband was keen to explain them to me and show how advantageous they were on a trip such as I was making. I listened with the sort of feigned interest that those of us who will never aspire to such luxuries do. It did not put him off, and he continued while his wife prepared supper. They had a cooker, pans and all the utensils required to eat in style. Whether these had been provided by the company with whom they were travelling or whether they had drawn upon their previous experiences and brought them from England I never learned, but I admired their organisation. They were not far off being as well organised and efficient as the ants I had observed some days before.

They had flown to Lyon and then cycled the 30 or so kilometres to the site as the first part of their journey. Their planned route took them in a circle around Lyon for a couple of weeks and then they were due to return to England. They had maps but did not seem to be part of a group, which surprised me. Perhaps others were elsewhere on the site, but I never learned of their existence.

They had all the equipment designed to make their fortnight's stay a Rolls Royce affair. They had cooling facilities, a stove, chairs that folded for ease of carrying on a bike and, what I envied most, they had a clothes line and clothes pegs! This was luxury and offered far better drying facilities than my attempts to hang wet clothes on the guide ropes of the tent, which led to me having to spend most of the day pulling them up after they had slipped to the ground. Occasionally, it was possible to attach a piece of string across from the tent to a neighbouring tree, but clothes pegs, phew! It had never occurred to me when packing that I would need such a simple device, but then there were other things that I could have brought that would also have been useful.

Next morning my neighbours were up in good time. The stove was on and the smell of fried bacon and sausage wafted over my tent. Little did they know the effect it was having on me. Their breakfast offered more sustenance than my bowl of cornflakes, especially for a hungry bike rider, though I have learned since that mine was the healthier diet. We continued the conversation we had had the previous evening, they letting me know how much they were looking forward to their journey of about 30 kilometres that day and how they were enjoying the French sunshine. They talked of their previous experiences and wondered how this would compare. They said how much they admired my efforts, but I must say they did not express their views with any outward show of enthusiasm. They did not learn the purpose of my journey, however, and the healing effects of the challenges that I had, and still had, to face. Before they left and cleared the last remnants of their breakfast, they offered me a coffee, which went down well with my biscuit and cemented our relationship. I was unable to offer them anything in return other than a '*bon voyage*'.

One thing I noticed about my fellow campers, especially those who somehow seemed to carry many of the 'luxuries' that I had not managed to bring, was the length of time it took them to pack in readiness for the next stage of their journey. I had seen it on other campsites: the meticulous packing designed to ensure no breakages; the care with which the tent was taken down and folded; the way in which tent pegs and hammer were put in the appropriate bag; and the businesslike way in which the bike was loaded. The efficiency again brought back to mind my friends the ants, though I could not recall ants having the time to enjoy the amount of discussion that was taking place here. It also reminded me of my shortcomings and what I needed to do if ever I was to make a similar journey again.

24 August 1997

DAY 24

Meyrieu les Etangs

Sunday is a day for lunch and pleasure for most of the French. For me it was a rest day. Judging by the number of spare seats at Mass, it is not a day for going to church for the large majority living in this area.

On my ride the previous day – again over 60 kilometres and one which had included the longest hill yet (7 kilometres) – I came across a new town of fascinating design. It being Sunday lunchtime, there were no French citizens anywhere and it looked absolutely dead. The design of the centre and the apartments was very different to the concrete blocks I often associate with new towns in England. Each apartment seemed to have its own character and to be designed to attract. They provided a feature that encouraged one to stay and look. The apartment blocks were not too tall and had interesting gabled roofs; they seemed to offer a degree of privacy that must have been welcomed by busy people returning from their places of business. The centre of the town contained a well-cared-for garden and the opportunity for a rest, which I took.

After a while I moved on, into more established territory which, surprisingly, was equally empty of people. It seemed that what I had seen confirmed the view that Sunday lunchtime, whether taken at home, in a restaurant or at some suitable place for a picnic, was sacred to the French. I have no doubt that they dined far longer than their English neighbours.

The only place I found open was a small bar which doubled as a bookmakers. This contained mainly men who were talking and drinking and clearly enjoying themselves. I ordered a drink and then noticed that suddenly everyone had gone very quiet. The television had captured everyone's attention and I could not help but join in. The bright colours of the jockeys sped across the screen with little to choose between them. Eventually, the race winners and the stakes were announced. It quickly became clear who among the watches had made the right choice as they went to the counter to collect their winnings. Among the others there were '*ha*'s' and '*ho*'s' and then the hubbub and the drinking restarted. I was not sure how this fitted into my understanding of the sacredness of France's Sunday lunch!

The barman spoke through the stub of what must have been, at one time, a cigar. He was continually lighting it, the result of his seeming to be chewing rather than puffing. He was too big for me to make any sort of comment, however, and had the sort of face designed for front-row forwards. We were in rugby territory. There were others in the bar who bore the same stamp of hard days on the field of play, several of them having ears that suggested that they had had to put their heads in places where no man should be expected to. There was the occasional lightweight, no doubt a winger or fly half, but all looked past their prime. The amount of smoke which filled the room suggested that if they were not, they should be.

My own encounters on the rugby field gave me an affinity with these guys and I appreciated what some of them must have been through. Fortunately, the scars I carried were hidden from view but as most rugger men would admit to, they were always there. I would have loved to talk to them about the games they played, the ones they won and lost, and shared my own stories of victories and defeats with them. Were it not for the language differences we could no doubt have had an enjoyable conversation. I knew that this area of France produced some of the best players and teams in the country and that players and supporters were proud of their achievements. I could not help but wonder whether, once the race results had been announced, their conversation drifted back to the glories of their playing days.

The lake and its environs were jam-packed by the time I returned to the campsite. I had passed many families sitting, as I had expected, at large tables under trees enjoying Sunday lunch or the siesta which follows. Everything was organised and indicated a regular habit. As usual, the women were in charge of the preparations for lunch while the men were in charge of the talking. It was so reminiscent of scenes I had seen by the river near my home. Most of those by the lake appeared to have brought lunch with them also and were settled in for the afternoon.

The lake's pleasures were well organised – entrance tickets, security guards and close supervision of the water activities. A portion of the lake was cordoned off for swimming and life guards were at the ready – but the main objective of most of the swimmers seemed to be to go beyond the cordon and swim the width of the lake. The signs on various parts of the bank, *Interdit baignade*, were totally ignored and nobody seemed to care. Was this a French approach to discipline or one that was international? I was not sure, but I could not imagine it happening in Germany, on the experience of my past visits. England? I remain doubtful.

Young and old were all over the lake. A soft brown hat over sun specs, seemingly deep in the water approached me at one stage, and I suddenly realised it was a guy older than me who was crocodile-like swimming round the lake, obviously looking for prey. In another instance a young boy who had already crossed the lake got into difficulties as he tried to get back to his family. It was a dangerous situation, one that almost encouraged me to dash to his aid. Fortunately, both of us were saved embarrassment by the arrival of the boy's father who helped him back across the lake. There were paddle-boats, canoes, rowing dinghies and sailboards, all ploughing waves between or seemingly over swimmers, creating what seemed to me to be a dangerous chaos. But enjoyment was universal.

I had decided to eat in the restaurant on the two days that I spent in this beautiful area. However, I had my usual problem with the restaurant staff. '*Une table pour un?*' I think the waiter said. '*Aujourd'hui monsieur*' and then I understood him to add 'inside, the restaurant is full, but you can have a quick snack on the terrace.'

As the quick snack turned out to consist of three courses, soup, main course and dessert, served by two pretty young ladies, my immediate disappointment was assuaged, though the price didn't seem any less than I thought I might have paid in the restaurant. The food was of good quality, well presented and obviously cooked to order. The taste was much better than at some restaurants where the food was pre-cooked and then re-heated so that hungry customers could be fed quickly and then encouraged to leave as quickly as possible so the table could be prepared for someone else. Not that this would have been the case in this establishment this evening, where trade, judging by the comings and goings of the waiters between the kitchens and the tables, seemed, what I understand is the jargon, slow. The terrace was well presented but clearly cut off from the main restaurant and its emptiness gave one the feeling of being a leper.

Eating on one's own is not a delight. I know that if Andrea had been with me we would have been found a table in the restaurant and enjoyed the atmosphere that is so important when eating out. The way the table would have been prepared, the candles, the choice of wine glasses and the general ambiance would, as had been our experience on previous occasions, have added a romantic element to the dinner. As it was, I was alone with my memories. I could not help but wonder if this experience was to be the story of my life henceforth.

On my visit on the second day the response was – '*Aujourd'hui monsieur*, the terrace is full but you can have a simple meal inside the restaurant. We have a table for one.'

The table for one was carefully placed in a corner, distant from the general hubbub of the rest of the diners. I could hear, but could see little. I did, however, feel some of the warmth that emanates from a good restaurant in which chatter and laughter are part of the scene. There is no doubt that the French enjoy their communal occasions as much if not more than the English and are not fazed by the presence of others. They talk loudly and seemingly consistently, only stopping to take a bite of food and chew it. From my point of view, the meal proved better than the quick snack, with more choice and coffee to finish with. However, how both meals compared with the full restaurant offering, I shall never know. Neither shall I know what cost I had avoided!

25 August 1997

DAY 25

Meyrieu les Etangs – Bourgoin-Jallieu –

La Tour du Pin – Les Abrets

The penultimate stage of my adventure. I was well ahead of my planned schedule, but a local newspaper had detailed coverage of the rowing event, one of the reasons for my journey: the course, the grandstands, the types of boats, a photo of the two key British oarsmen who had ruled the world for almost a decade as *le grand attraction*, and a programme of events. To my surprise, the racing started on Sunday. I had expected it to be Monday, which, if my memory had served me right, was the normal starting day.

My original carefully planned journey was designed to get me to the championships by the Saturday, so that I would have time to meet with those members of my family and friends who were making the journey by a different means of transport to mine. It was also geared to enable me to settle into a hotel and put behind me some of the more uncomfortable experiences of my journey. As it was, my progress had been so far ahead of the plan that I now expected to arrive on the Wednesday previous to the championships. In many respects, this was a good time to arrive and a target date that I could have usefully set myself as the national rowing teams would already be assembling to acclimatise themselves and learn the vagaries of the course they were to row. I would have a good opportunity to see their final preparations, comparing their readiness to that of my own crews who had taken on the world on previous occasions.

The art of the sportsman or sportswoman, whatever the sport, is to 'peak' at the right time. There is little point in 'bossing' the event through a season if, when the crunch comes, all the required energies have been spent. Much the same applies to those who build more slowly, keeping an eye on the key dates when they needed to raise their performance, only to find the opportunity has gone and their best is still to come. This is what makes the week of preparation and the week of the races in rowing so fascinating, and why I was delighted to have arrived a little earlier than expected. The psychology involved in preparing a crew is of the utmost importance and an aspect in which the coach of *le grand attraction* was a past master. Having developed his knowledge and skills in Eastern Europe, Jergen Grobler had brought, to my club Leander and Great Britain rowing, a different perspective to training and race motivation, based on coaching Olympic gold medal crews for twenty years. He knew how medals could be won and less about how they might be lost. This is why his crews had such confidence in his methods and were unlikely to falter on the day of the race. They knew they would be ready! For my part, on this occasion I had gone no further than thinking of the bed I might sleep in. I had almost forgotten what it would be like to sleep in a bed again.

This campsite was four-star luxury, but like many, miles from anywhere. It was also surrounded by hills, some of them providing a challenge even to accomplished cyclists such as I. At least, such a description was one which I was now proudly boasting to myself. Little was I to know at this point that I had more to learn! I prided myself on making the journey without having had to get off my bike at even the steepest hill, other than when I surrendered in the mountains near Rocamadour, and the decision I made, which I was now beginning to regret. A retreat down the Dordogne valley, another battle with the *moustiques* and the likelihood of travelling in better weather would have meant a significant detour, but would have enabled me to find more passable roads and continue on my bike. My consolation was the memory of the generosity of my

147

fellow traveller struggling with me to lift the bike on and off the train despite the prospect of a severe rupture.

In a car, distances are minimal, but a hilly ride on a bike – and there were plenty of respectable hills around this site – meant that an 8 kilometre ride became a challenge, which I had not yet grown used to totally. Nevertheless, brave as I am, I decided it was better to go in search of a nice cool beer in the country rather than hang around the campsite. What a mistake! The hills were such that I moved quickly from aerobic to anaerobic, from steady breathing to almost uncontrollable panting, after only a short distance. I could not resist the question, 'How is this after I have previously covered almost 1,600 kilometres of road and taken most hills in my stride?' With sweat dripping off the end of my nose and dryness in my throat, I found it difficult to order the drink I had travelled 8 kilometres to get. There is little wonder that the barman looked amused at this Englishman who thought himself a cyclist.

It is not surprising that most people stuck to the campsite, on which there was much to do. There were swimming pools, games areas and special provision for the youngest children. There were also plenty of eating and drinking places. For some people, hiking offered an attractive pastime and some had clearly come with this in mind. They were kitted with appropriate footwear, knapsacks, and several with alpine walking sticks. Some had maps of the area and left the site with that confidence of the well-prepared and seasoned walker. It was as if they were saying to me 'If you do not want to ride, walk'.

As a matter of fact I like walking. I find it similar in many ways to cycling. In the one, you have to concentrate on pressing one pedal down after the other, especially when the route gets tough, and in the other you have to think of the next step, especially as tiredness sets in. Interestingly enough, I find walking very therapeutic, an exercise that keeps my mind unobtrusively active. On my second day, having decided that my bike needed a rest, I set out on a longish walk of about 10 kilometres. The countryside was beautiful, the stone farmhouses almost glowing in the sun. The birds were plentiful and noisily protecting their claims. The cows were at ease, either shading under trees or lying down as only cows can. There were no 'moos' though plenty of chewing of cud. What satisfaction and what peace of soul they displayed. Sheep were plentiful and were continuing to nibble blade after blade, as if their challenge was, like conquerors of old, to devastate the field they were attacking by evening.

I could not help but reflect on the relationship the French have with their livestock – not so much their dogs, this time – but their cows, their cockerels, their ducks and their geese. For example, to see a huge gaggle of several hundred geese in the Dordogne being herded (if that's the right word) back from pasture and then the one or two in the backyard, which were there presumably for local consumption, was fascinating. They received great care and attention, but were bred, like all farm animals for a specific purpose. I had seen women, who seemed as comfortable as men in what they were about, something less noticeable in England I thought, deciding which rabbit was suitable for tea, catching it and doing the honours without a qualm. Animal rights there were but only in so far as they were understood within the need for food.

My next reflection was on the seasonal invasion of France by the Dutch. There were colonies of them on all the better class sites. I had heard of their presence in Scotland and Ireland where they were beginning to buy property, but here, in France, they seemed to be everywhere, greatly outnumbering the Germans and the British I had come across. Their great strength was their organisation, their tidiness and their obvious enjoyment of the life with friends on the campsite. I also began to think of the rowers gathering at Lac Aiguebelette, looking forward with excitement to the challenge of the competition, and could not help hoping that the lads and lasses I had helped in some small way over several years through coaching would have success.

I could not help but reflect on my family. I thought of my grandson's birthday, which was close at hand, and how we men often think of birthdays simply in terms of the seventh, the ninth,

149

the twenty-first and so on, rather than in terms of the pain, excitement and pleasure of the actual birth. To me, that has become the real meaning of a birthday. My wife never had an easy birth and she always took time to recover, whether it be from the physical, as with stitches, which was the case with our first baby, Alison, who had to be pulled out with forceps, or the psychological, that is with concerns for the health of the babies. I regard myself as being fortunate in that our children were born in those days when husbands were not expected to be present at a birth. I have never envied my sons' 'pleasure' at being present at their own children's births. Indeed, I was only informed of the birth of my younger son by telephone at about 2.00 am and, to my embarrassment and the amusement of the nurse, I had to ring next morning to ask whether I had been dreaming or whether a son was a reality. Needless to say, this caused great amusement among the nurses and the other mothers-to-be in my wife's ward, and led to my being serenaded with 'Rock-a-bye Baby' or something to that effect as I walked down to my wife's bed.

From looking back on such innocence my meditations became concerned with the hopes and aspirations that Andrea and I had for the children and to what extent they had been realised. It was inevitable that I began to think about the growing family. Many of the things I had seen on this trip brought back memories. I had seen families on holiday, camping, filling the car with children and camping paraphernalia, laughing, crying and arguing, the one giving way to the other. I had passed French families living seemingly kilometres from anywhere but giving the aura of closely-knit units inhabiting a cottage surrounded by fields and both domestic and farm animals. I had seen families at restaurant tables, debating what to have and from table to table seeing the sausage and *frites* at 15 francs translate into the 90 francs menu, depending on the apparent prosperity of the family. My journey had taken me by families organised and disorganised as they packed away or pitched tents, the activities of those seeking their time in the sun.

All these things and many more are part of family life. I could not escape it. My own family had had its joys and sorrows, its achievements and failures, but it was a family. It was a family that was held together primarily by my wife's dedication to our children and to me. It is for this and many more things that I felt it worth lighting a candle.

26 August 1997

DAY 26

Les Abrets

Another rest day, or supposedly. I was not one for sitting about the campsite for the sake of it, especially as there was often little to do for a man of my age, especially if he was on his own. There were usually facilities for children, such as swings and roundabouts, and others in the family always seemed to have plenty to do, whether it be chatting or doing the usual camping chores; washing clothes, preparing for the next meal, checking that all was well with the tent. When families were staying a few days it did not take long for children and adults to find like-minded campers who were willing to play, to exchange stories about the journey or about life in general, and to share a drink.

Some years previously, on one campsite, deep in the south of France, where the family was staying for several days I remember being invited by Frenchmen from neighbouring tents to play *boules* with them. They had seen my interest as I sat outside the tent quietly watching them and occasionally returning a *boule* which had lost its way. I joined in with enthusiasm, but my *boule* was about as good as my French, and it showed. I had good teachers, however, and after two or three days both were improving. It was the most fruitful contact that I had had with the French on that or any other trip until this one. For her part, Andrea, who spoke French more confidently than I, enjoyed comparing the French way of life with the English during her conversations with a lively group of French women. On my present site no opportunity for me to become involved in this way offered itself and so I dreamed up the idea of going for a bike ride. What did Noel Coward write about 'Mad dogs and Englishmen'?

Without realising it, I was in terrain that was mainly hilly, or even mountainous when comparing the height of these hills to those in England. What I did see when I looked at the map was a lake, a place, no doubt, where I might find some entertainment. To reach it, however, looked a challenge, as it was nestled within surrounding hills. No matter, I managed to find a road which went in the general direction, a road that took me up what I would describe as a mountain! To be fair, I think it was a relatively small mountain, but it took some climbing. Up and up and up, bend after bend the road climbed, leading me I knew not where. I could not help asking myself why I had chosen to do this, but could find no answer. The spectacles were off, the nose was dripping and the lowest gear possible in operation. Cars passed both ways, and to hear those going in the same direction as I was, changing gear not once but twice, moved the spirit. The tendency when climbing under pressure is to allow the bike to wobble from side to side, a dangerous practice on this road which had its fair share of cars. I had to concentrate to avoid wandering into the middle of the road and then back towards the verge, moving like some drunkard after a night's outing. As I had managed to do throughout my journey, however, I persisted and at last reached the top to find myself in a land of hill farms and well-kept houses.

The grass was green in many places and the houses were surrounded by resplendent flower pots and flower beds. I wondered what winter held for places at this height and how long the beauty that was now entrancing me lasted. I could not believe that I would find such tranquillity. It was time to stop and enjoy – to think of the delightful Dales in Yorkshire and the Cotswolds in Gloucestershire. So much that I could see was reminiscent of these places and the summer days I spent with Andrea breathing in, as we would say, 'the warmth and peacefulness for winter'. I suspect few non-French cars saw this territory, their drivers not knowing what they were passing by.

The sweep down the other side was less steep and controllable and brought me to my destination for the day – Le Lac Palladon. It had all the trappings of the lake that I had seen from my campsite two days previously, but this was Tuesday, not Saturday or Sunday. Consequently, it was mainly deserted and many of the 'beach' areas looked shabby now that they were empty. It is amazing how areas soon look uncared-for and unkempt once the hordes of people have gone, only to come alive again when they return. Half a dozen French were having a picnic under a tree, seemingly enjoying themselves in the solitude that compared so starkly with the excitement of the weekends. The restaurant was quiet but two or three French were having *frites* with something and were as garrulous as ever. I decided that I deserved a beer, though the perspiration of the journey had now disappeared and the tiredness had not yet crept into my bones. Mind you, I had a pizza and *tarte aux pommes* in my saddlebag for later, though where I was going to warm the pizza remained a mystery.

The journey back to the campsite was nowhere near as stressful as the outward journey, as the steepest of the climbs was now downhill. I made the return in half the time. Once at the campsite I had my usual evening shower, an event that brought home to me how important sanitary arrangements are and how one has to adjust to those on a campsite.

What campsites have to offer varies enormously. The big difference between the good and not so good, for me, is the arrangement for carrying out one's ablutions. This is something I had forgotten during the past few years, the result of the children leaving home and Andrea and I being able to afford something a little more comfortable. When you visit over 20 sites in a month, however, you are again faced with stark reality. Fortunately, the Michelin guide does indicate the quality of facilities through its quality system and most of the sites I visited provided well. Much has been done since my early camping days in the 1950s. Even so, you cannot escape the fact that sanitary arrangements are communal – I should have used a big 'C'. There were very few that I had visited on this trip where there was any distinction made for men and women, resulting in both sexes entering and leaving the same loos and showers. On one occasion this found me in one shower with a fine bottle of high-quality body massage which had been forgotten – I must say it was toning my skin up marvellously when a female voice suddenly floated over the door asking if there was a bottle of de luxe massage on the shelf. The hand that followed obviously knew there was and grasped the bottle that I placed in it before quickly disappearing. Gone was my toning, but at least half my body had that sensuous feel about it that the lady was seeking to use to attract the males as she moved around the campsite. I hesitated to think what my luck might be.

The only area which seemed strictly reserved for men was the *pissoir*. I think that is what they are called. I remember the excitement caused by the placement of one in the square in front of the bank in that classic French story *Clochemerle*. On a campsite, they appear not to cause any consternation. Sometimes they are outside, hidden by hip-high fencing, sometimes in a corner inside the main toilet block, and on a couple of occasions I observed them directly outside the shower area, used by men and women, with no protection whatsoever. I don't know what women think and for that matter what men think about that last situation. I know that some men appear shy in an all-men's loo, conspicuously guarding the sight of their penis from the eyes of everyone else, so how they cope in these situations is beyond my comprehension. I suppose the option is to use the WC all the time. This can also be a problem, especially if the campsite uses the term WC for the French style feet in the snow toilet.

When I have made the mistake, twice on this trip, of interpreting WC to mean the English type of toilet and found myself in the French type I did not escape on either occasion without wet feet. On one occasion, I opened the door first, ready to jump out as soon as I had pulled the belt which was serving as a replacement chain. Pull and jump I said to myself, practising the movement. Well the movement went OK, but I still succeeded in wetting myself and in addition the area outside which was within close vicinity to the loo. Mind you, many French are no better with the traditional English WC, seemingly having difficulties in finding what to press, push or pull to flush them. The site guardians do a magnificent job in keeping on top of this aspect of their work, making sure that the loos are cleaned regularly and attending to any problems that might arise during the day.

The improvements in sanitary arrangements which I noticed on this trip were particularly noticeable in the quality of the showers. The cubicles are usually of a good size and in the most up-to-date include a separate washbasin, mirror, stool and guarded hanging space. Even here, though, the designers have not yet found a way to stop idiots like me getting their footwear wet. In most showers the shower head is immovably fixed to the back of the wall. From this position it can and does succeed in spraying anything on the floor within the cubicle. In my early experiences, if I went in trainers, which I usually did, I might as well have worn them while showering. My natural inclination was to slide them off and push them into a corner, well out of harm's way, as I thought it, whilst I showered. The system defeated me initially, however, as the all-enveloping water spread around the lower part of the cubicle and the trainers were wet through in seconds. One counteraction I developed, which succeeded in defeating the shower, was to push my footwear through the gap at the bottom of the cubicle so that it was mostly in the next cubicle. This worked well until '*Quel dommage!*' – half way through my shower someone started to shower in the other cubicle, paying little attention to my once-dry trainers. I tramped through the site back to my tent squelching at every step.

One designer had obviously given a great deal of thought to this problem and created a small partition on which the showerhead was fixed, which helped to point the flow of water away from anything hanging on the walls or in the opposite corner. This was designed to keep clothes and footwear dry. His ingenuity was doomed to failure, however. The spray was strong enough to hit the back wall and rebound onto the floor in the opposite corner exactly where my trainers were positioned, whilst the water continued to bounce off my body into the same area. In the best showers there was a second partition which allowed the camper to hang clothes behind it and away from the spraying of water. This inclusive partition was also a useful idea, providing, as it did, protection for clothing. For most people this, I guessed, worked well. For me, there was also a 'but'. On one occasion, for instance, when reaching round the partition for my soap, which I had left on the shelf, I knocked my shorts off the hanger and left the shower not only with wet feet, but also with a wet bum.

Despite what I have said about campsites, there is no doubt that this one at Les Abrets, Le Coin Tranquil, had much in its favour. It was beautifully situated, surrounded as it was by mountains and having ready access to a variety of lakes. It had a large and well-staffed restaurant, required for the number of campers and caravanners that were using the site. There was also plenty to do for families; the site had two pools and facilities for tennis, archery and so on. Little wonder that it was so busy.

27 August 1997

DAY 27

Les Abrets – Le Pont de Beauvoisin – Lac Aiguebelette

Today was the day that I expected to reach the end of my journey on my revised plan. In my mind was the phrase 'objective achieved!' I could not believe that I would finally make it to the lake, but with a fair wind I would. But of course this was only part of the objective and not the most important. There is no doubt that I had been enthused by the challenge of cycling round most of France, cycling more kilometres than I had ever dreamed of even as a young man. It gave me a sense of achievement to look back on my adventures and recognise that I had managed to cover over 1600 kilometres of sometimes difficult terrain without mishap. I had not fallen off the bike, grazed an elbow or met with any really unsavoury characters throughout my adventure. The roads had, in the main, been kind to me and the French helpful when the need arose.

Lac Aiguebelette means 'beautiful little waters' and it is one of France's natural lakes. Situated among mountains it benefits from a wind shadow, which makes it ideal for rowing. The prohibition of motor boats means that the water keeps its natural colour and is not polluted with the likes of oil spillage. It is a delightful spot and one well known to French holidaymakers.

However, reaching the lake was not the main purpose. The key reason for my trip was to allow me to grieve in a way different to the norm. Although it was 12 months since Andrea had passed away I still suffered from that sense of loss and loneliness that nestle in the mind when a loved one is no longer there. And still the question, 'Why her? Why had she, like so many others, had to suffer as she did when there was a God in heaven? How could these things be explained?'

I had, it is true, used my work to help me accept what had become inevitable and overcome what might be called the superficial grief, the grief that everyone expects you to show but bear. So many admire you if you seem to get on with your responsibilities as quickly and normally as possible. In my case I rarely shed tears or, I hope, look for sympathy. To outsiders, and even those close to me, I suspect they believed I was coping well and that I was of that ilk who could take such a pain in his stride. What they did not see was that deep grief that is forever present, which does not allow one to forget loved ones or think of them without pangs of anguish. It was an attempt to deal with this inner grief that had led to the journey and my first and most important objective, the lighting of a candle to Andrea's memory. Today was the day on which the challenge had been successfully met, that my grief was assuaged to an extent beyond what simply following a 'normal life' could have done, and finally on which the candle was to be lit.

I chose the last church I was likely to see on my approach to Lac Aiguebelette. It had no particularly significant features. It was a parish church which served the needs of the locality and no doubt had provided help and support for others who had lost a dear one. I passed through the porch and pushed the door. It opened allowing the scent, which I had grown so accustomed to over the many years I had practised my faith, to impact on my senses. It was not of flowers, of which there were many adorning the altar, but of incense. A scent similar to that which had surrounded my beloved wife as her final Mass on earth came to an end. I made the sign of the cross with the water from the small font by the door, genuflected and knelt in a pew before the altar. Much about the church was as I expected and which would have made my wife feel at ease; to the left of the altar a statue of the Virgin Mary, to the right the Sacred Heart. Central was the tabernacle, which contained the Blessed Sacrament.

My prayers were reflective, thanking Our Lord for the time Andrea and I had spent together, sometimes with the family, sometimes just together; thanking Him for the faith that we had shared and which had given a purpose to our lives and a special meaning to family; and thanking Him for the love he had bestowed on us. I could not help but thank Him for Andrea's conversion to Catholicism, a surprise and joy to me, and the commitment she had shown thereafter and the example which she had set me. These and many more thoughts ran through my head as I prayed for Andrea and all the others, who I did not know, who had found their final peace in this church.

The candles were situated at the foot of Our Lady's statue, in a small side altar. It was here that my major objective was accomplished and it was from this place that I could journey with more peace of mind than at any other time since my wife's death. The bond that we had celebrated almost 40 years ago was cemented further in my mind through this simple act of placing a prayerful candle before Our Lord's mother.

At precisely 12.00 pm I had my first glimpse of the turquoise blue water which was to be home to the World Championships over the coming week. I had conquered all the hills put in my way, though I have to admit often through judicious use of the Michelin maps and their indicative arrows > < showing the steepness of a climb or a descent. The final hill, at the foot of which stood the church, was to be today. It was arrowed, but successfully overcome, with the usual sweat and guts.

There were a lot of campsites around the lake, some seemingly running down to the shore and presumably giving access to swimming. Many looked incredibly overcrowded and cheap. This was a holiday area and it was clear that the last of the holidaymakers were taking what advantage they could of the few summer days that remained. Their numbers were now being swelled by the first of the rowing supporters, and for me the place began to have that bit of buzz such a major event needed. A few teams had already arrived, I saw a women's coxless four from Canada on the water for instance, but the course was on the far side of the lake, too distant to pick out individuals in crews, and mainly cut off from supporters just wanting to watch.

No accreditation means no access to non-oarsmen or non-oarswomen to those parts of the lake that were beginning to come alive with the voices of coxes and the sound of oars as the powerful crews drew them through the water, leaving pools behind, which indicated how well they were going. The further the stern of the boat was beyond the last pool that was made by the oar of the bowman, usually the lightest of the crew, the better the boat was travelling. As always on these occasions, whilst their crews are on the water, coaches seem to become superfluous, because they are too far from the course to make their shouting voices heard and they are not allowed to use anything like a megaphone. However, they watch, sometimes with binoculars, to check on the placement of the blades, the rhythm of the crew and how well movement is synchronised. Everything was designed to enable them to make those technical and tactical adjustments once the crew was off the water that could make the difference between medals and disappointments.

My site overlooked the boating area, but from there I had yet to see any of the rowers I was likely to recognise. My best hope was to take a seemingly casual walk along the side of the lake. By chance, I met the Fosters, parents of one of the British coxless four. They had just finished dinner in a nearby hotel – how lucky some can be – and were also taking a stroll. We chatted, I learned a little more about the plans of the British team and the hopes for medals and then we parted.

I became aware that what had been a warm and balmy evening was changing and the dark clouds drifting from the west were threatening rain. My experience on my journey told me that once it had decided to rain it did so with enthusiasm. I quickened my pace, dodged between groups of oarsmen, sometimes having to duck under their blades as they carried them back to their headquarters, and arriving back at the site installed my tent as quickly as possible. No sooner was the job finished than the heavens opened. Fortunately I had found a protected spot under a large tree for my bike, which I could just see through the gap in the doorway, and had managed to get inside the tent all those things likely to be ruined by water. I settled in for the night, looking forward to the next day.

What an optimist I am! The rain was still coming down 12 hours later with no signs of it abating. On the twenty-eighth day I was trapped in my tent at 9.30 am with little prospect of escape. I was desperate for the loo, not unusual first thing in the morning, and I had heard the *boulanger* come and go with my anticipated breakfast still in his van. At that time I had no answer to the rain but to stay put, hold my breath and dream of a croissant. If I went out I had to try to dress, with the danger of touching the tent walls and creating something similar to a watery grave. If I succeeded in getting out, I would be wet through in seconds, with the prospect of bringing water back into the tent via sodden clothes, body and feet. Even if I went outside, the only place I could go was the loo ('Oh please, stop raining', just to think of the loo brought anguish), because there was no other shelter either on the site or anywhere else as far as I could judge outside the hotels.

The main thing now was to pass the time and hope that the water stopped coming down outside before it started oozing inside. I worked at passing time. I read the blurb that I had collected at the tourist office about the campsite and the wonderful Pays Savoyard, both without and with the aid of my French dictionary. I counted sheep, I reminisced and I rearranged the 'furniture' inside the tent so that I could make a quick break for it if the rain abated. But by midday it was still raining! I was almost tempted to peep outside to see if it was just raining on me rather than the rest of the site and that the area around, including the lake was bathed in sunlight. Or could I be imagining it all? 'Splat, splat and splat' – no I didn't think so.

The fateful time came. I was bursting. I had to go. Getting pyjamas off and a semblance of clothes on in a one-man tent without touching the sides and encouraging water to drip in requires either a very small person or a contortionist. As I am neither, I had some anxious moments. Trying to get my pyjama jacket off, for instance, had me twisting and turning, almost wrenching my arm out at one point metaphorically hopping from foot to foot whilst trying to get out of a straitjacket. I kept wondering where Houdini kept his spare key. Getting shorts on was easier but then opening up the front brought water cascading down my arm. No matter, towel and washing kit under my arm I made a dash for the loo. I had some gratification in seeing that it was raining on everybody else too, and that I had the sanitation block to myself. Thank goodness I did not have to wait for a loo, even though they were of the French design. Having a shower seemed pointless in light of what I had just experienced but as a creature of habit I could not resist. One thing was for sure, it would not matter if the shower was so designed to wet everything in the cubicle. Feeling somewhat refreshed I now had to get back to my tent, which I did with all speed. Splat, splat and splat; nothing had changed.

It was 2.30 pm. I heard a bird sing, to be joined by others, as though they were making up for the dawn chorus. I also heard a voice, though it was moving apace. These were indicators that the rain may have gone or at least was easing. The fact that I was under a tree, believe it or not to shade me from the sun, did not help because the leaves kept shedding water. Voices are always a good sign, however, and they were becoming more frequent. At 3.00 pm I emerged, again encouraged by nature, and saw the sun beginning to peep out of wispy clouds. Day had come at last.

At 4.00 pm I had my first sight of the British team as they arrived. A few nods to old acquaintances was as much contact as I could make, as the rowers were clearly intent on other things and stiffening their attitude in readiness for what was to come.

By chance I met my friends whom I had seen the previous evening and spent an hour talking with them. Their son was in the coxless four, a favoured boat, and they were hopeful of a good

163

medal. Their nervousness, or was it anticipation, showed, but so many fathers and mothers had been in their position, sometimes fruitfully, sometimes disappointedly. As is the case when oldies get together we discussed the rights and wrongs of selection, the appointment of coaches and the likely strength of the opposition. We had no difficulty in putting the world to rights, especially now that the Championships were beginning to take shape. We parted, they to their swish restaurant and caravan, me to my wet tent and cold fare.

28 August 1997

DAY 28

Aiguebelette

The rain continued through the night but had abated by morning. I would be able to breakfast outside once I had the necessary sustenance. I was able to avail myself of the *boulanger*'s van and acquire a croissant and those lovely chocolate–filled buns they make. This morning was to be a feast. Out came the stove, the pan and the water. The match lit without trouble, the stove followed and coffee was on the way. I enjoyed sitting by the tent, on the ground of course and without the pleasures that those in caravans with their plush seats, or so it seemed to me, enjoyed. There was enough sun to give warmth and to encourage me to linger over breakfast. I could not help but reflect on my days on the road and what it had taken to get me here. When I set out my thoughts were still clouded by the memories of Andrea and I did not foresee my ride as being anything extraordinary. It was a challenge, sure enough, but nothing had really prepared me for the adventure. Now, however, my experiences over the last few weeks were helping to clear my mind and to encourage me to think more positively about my future.

Andrea would be forever in my thoughts; we had shared too much, and our four children would be a constant reminder of many of those happy occasions. For their part, I could foresee that they would want to talk with me and to one another about their 'mum'. What had happened had been no easier for them than it had been for me. Although we had shared so many things and all enjoyed together many special moments of family life, they had also, as I had, their own experiences with their 'mum', experiences that I probably never knew about.

It is strange how families operate as a unit for much of the time, with mum and dad, each with a different role, as the figureheads. Within that unit, however, each member gathers his or her own memories, has his or her own experiences, and in some ways leads a separate life. It is in this way that the family blossoms as these different experiences are shared and joint recollections recounted. There is little doubt that in better times the different interpretations on the same happenings had caused much merriment around the table at lunch or tea. It was only later, in the months after Andrea's death that I learned more and more about my children, about their relationships with their 'mum' and their views on me.

In her last days Andrea spent much time talking about the importance of family and the mutual support we could provide for one another. She had been right of course, and it was from family relationships that I was to gain the strength I needed. It was not surprising, therefore, that I waited with eagerness for the day on which my children and grandson were due to arrive at Aiguebelette for the championships and which would provide the opportunities to talk about the future.

For my part, I felt at this moment that the ride had fulfilled its purpose. It had helped me come to terms with the loss of Andrea, to recognise the reality of my situation and to encourage me to look forward with hope as well as back with love and sadness. The memories were critically important, and, along with my children, would serve to provide the strength to face the future. The candle marked a new beginning.

The site was beginning to fill not only with tents but with different languages. German, Dutch, Spanish, and a range of what I took to be Eastern European, mingled with French and English. It made me wonder about the Apostles in the Upper Room and the ability blessed upon them to be able to speak in many different languages. I could appreciate how those Jews of one language were mesmerised when the Apostles emerged and communicated with whomever they wished. I imagine they felt like I did and relied on a nod now and again, pretending to understand at least something of what was being said. Above all, the site had a spirit of companionship, with different individuals, families and groups intermingling as best they could. Not surprisingly, English became the most common language and so I was able to contribute to conversations going on in neighbouring tents. The ability of other Europeans, especially the Dutch, to speak English continues to amaze me and explains why so few Britons feel the need to master a foreign language.

By mid-morning I was again as close to the lake as I could get, hoping to see rowers and coaches I knew and, as best I could, observe the techniques of those I did not. In fact, activity that morning was very limited and there was little to keep me. I wended my way back to the campsite, avoiding boats and oars, which always seem bigger and more unwieldy out of the water than on it, as they were being carried to their racks for the week by the oarsmen and women. Apart from the odd nod I made little contact with men and women whose opponents I had spent many an hour coaching, no matter what the weather.

By the time I arrived back at my tent the weather looked promising and so, as usual, I decided to use my rest day to go for a bike ride. I looked at the map and planned a 30 to 40 kilometre sojourn through what looked like wooded terrain. Once on the bike, the ride offered a very pleasant interlude before the excitement of the racing and a period of stillness and quietness which I enjoyed. I had no destination to reach or constriction of time, and so I was able to take note of what was about me. Very few cars passed in either direction, and the swish of bike wheels passing over the smooth tarmac road did not disturb my listening to what I thought to be blackbirds and thrushes, as well as a variety of finches, and the occasional rustle of the leaves above as they caught the slight breeze. I cycled at a steady pace, well within my capabilities, suc-

167

cessfully avoiding the panting and sweating of earlier days. I was feeling pretty fit and ready for anything. Or so I thought.

Without warning I suddenly found myself on a steep downward road. It had appeared unexpectedly and caught me unprepared. Before I knew what was happening I was travelling at a pace that made it difficult to negotiate the bends or use my brakes without danger of bringing the bike to a shuddering halt and its rider splayed somewhere over the front wheels. For the first time on my journey I felt pangs of panic. I looked for ways of escape as the bike continued to gather speed and I felt my control slipping. My stomach welled up into my mouth and the stupidity and danger of the situation in which I found myself, after so many kilometres of safe riding, astounded me. My only recourse was the grass verge, which, fortunately, was of some width and low in relation to the road. I made the decision, headed off the road, hit the verge and found myself in a bush. The bike was on its side, wheels spinning furiously, as I disentangled myself, hoping to find no blood or other sign of injury. I was in luck. So was the bike. But we both had had a scare we would not want to repeat. Certainly, this was a story not to be told to anyone I met, as much as a result of the embarrassment as my inability to explain it.

Once I had brushed myself down, bent at the knees to check on my mobility and then checked the bike I decided to walk back up the hill and head for the safety of the campsite. The experience had been a chastening one and I hoped not to repeat it.

When I reached the campsite, all was as I had left it. Campers were doing their chores, sitting talking or checking on the security of their pitch. I offered the usual nods and was pleased to get to my tent, make safe my bike and crawl onto my sleeping bag. I had managed a sandwich for lunch but had used too many calories for that to satisfy me for the rest of the day. As a result, once I had rested and the pangs of hunger began, I decided to venture out in search of a decent restaurant. Aiguebelette did not offer a great deal, but, as is usual when crowds begin to gather, plenty of snack-bar-type places had begun to appear. They did not pretend to offer gourmet French cooking, but what they did offer was sufficient to entice me and satisfy my hunger. I was still disappointed not to have made contact with, or even seen, any members of the national squad. I assumed that they would have arrived by now and would be acclimatising to the conditions, not only in terms of weather but also in relation to the lake on which they were to row. I knew the head coach well enough to know that he would not leave anything to chance.

I had learned the previous evening that friends of mine, the Redgraves, were camping on a site a short distance from my own. I knew them well and felt the need to go for a chat and so cycled across to talk to them about the championships and their son Steven, probably the greatest oarsmen ever. We spent a pleasant hour and then it was time to leave. I made my way back to the campsite. Bustle was still about the place as new people arrived and others enthusiastically prepared themselves for the big event. I tidied around and inside my tent, the experience of my travels warning me that the weather could not be trusted, and then prepared for bed.

29 August 1997

DAY 29

Aiguebelette

I awoke to find it had rained during the night. By 8.45 am it was raining again. I recognised that my camping expedition was coming to a sodden end. The weather forecast had been for much sun, but the way things were that hope seemed destined to be frustrated. This did not surprise me, as I had become used to weather forecasts in different parts of the world and come to the conclusion that the best way to treat them was 'to wait and see'. Still there were compensations in the situation in which I found myself. I used my French grammar book to learn a few more French words and even some of the grammar to go with them. I felt confident that if I were to start my journey again I would be able to converse and find answers to the many questions I had wanted to ask as I passed through Normandy, Anjou, Poitiers and the different parts of France.

Another benefit, more pertinent to my current situation, was the skill I was developing to enable me to take off my sandals at the door of the tent whilst trying to avoid the rain and making sure I crawled into the tent reasonably dry. I was improving but I still had some way to go. I had accepted that I would have wet sandals, because they had to be left outside, which meant wet feet the next time I put them on, and a wet bum as I manoeuvred myself head first into the tent. This was the West of Scotland and the Lake District all over again, but without the company of those I loved.

The sun did shine eventually, but fitfully, and the mornings and evenings were certainly becoming 'fresh' if not cold – partially the result of the campsite being amidst the mountains and partially the result of a disappearing summer. The proprietor of the campsite spent ten minutes each morning writing the weather forecast carefully on a whiteboard. She was keen to supply an on-the-spot service for her campers. She was also keen to keep abreast of any changes, which meant three different forecasts for today. I was left wondering whether she was imagining the forecast, recording it, in French of course, as she saw it – rain followed by hazy sunshine; sun followed by rain; rain with prospect of sun tomorrow – or watching different channels on the television. Whatever, her summaries seemed to coincide with the immediate rather than with the future and offered little as a forecast.

The prospect of sun encouraged me to take the risk of unhitching my bike and making for the nearby village of Novalaise. I discovered it was well protected by a demanding hill, which was likely to dissuade me making another visit, but I found much to admire. Well-established houses with gardens to match gave the village the look of being well cared for. The square had the characteristics of many French villages, with its neighbouring church and village hall. It was clearly a meeting place to which locals would be attracted. The busy café bore witness to that, though most of the clients clearly favoured the dry of the interior to the uncertainty of the weather on the terrace. The villagers were polite though I did not stop to chatter. My confidence in my French, which I had been lauding earlier in the day, evaporated as soon as I heard '*Bonjour monsieur, comment allez-vous?*', or some enquiry equally innocent. I continued my ride and went round the other side of the lake to my camp, a route which had one or two dips and climbs, but which found me quietly singing to myself as I realised I was not going to get wet.

Washing laundry on a campsite for someone like me brings yet another challenge. Taking advantage of *madame's* update of sun for later in the day I scurried over to the washing machine, keen to beat the competition. Unfortunately, washers come in different sizes and shapes, and with seemingly incomprehensible directions as to how to get them started. In this case, I needed a *jeton* from the bureau, a task that took a while to negotiate, the result of the conversation with *madame* being half in French, which was my weak link, and half in English, which was hers. Once success had been achieved, I had the task of reading the instructions on how to make the machine work. I understood enough to get my clothes into the washer and was then helped out by another camper who showed commendable expertise in switching the machine on. I watched the clothes go round and round as one does when there is little else to do. I saw the soap suds appear, then disappear as water took over, a repetition, and then heard a gushing of water as the washer emptied.

With washing in my arms I went to look for a clothes line. My only recourse was to approach *madame*. Instantaneously it seemed as though she knew what I wanted, which was not surprising in view of my load. The problem was the next step. It took ten minutes of arm waving, eyes rolling, and an almost new vocabulary of Anglo-French words resembling Esperanto before I was left as confused as when we started. It was only when I walked round the back of the bureau that I saw what I think had been referred to, the home clothes line. No matter, that was where my clothes were hung and with pegs which were described to me with forefingers and thumb opening and closing like a duck's mouth.

Sometime later when I went to retrieve my clothes, I was offered, I assume by the gesticulations which reminded me of the nursery rhyme song, an iron and ironing board. Knowing that my clothes were going to be screwed up and rammed into pannier bags and not wanting another prolonged word game, I found the word *non* very useful. I felt I had done enough to meet my daughters' commands to wash my clothes weekly.

I had dinner that evening with the English family and pleasant it was. They are turning out to be English lessons for the waiters, however, for which we are not being paid. '*C'est un poisson*, how do you say in English, it is a . . . ?' was not an uncommon start to a new course.

172

Tonight I faced the prospect of my last night in the tent. I had been sleeping under canvas for a month, something which I had not intended to do and something which my children would have dissuaded me from if they had known. Their concern would have been my safety; mine, as usual, came down to cost. As I have said before, there is something about coming from Yorkshire that encourages 'thriftiness'. Certainly it was an art I had developed during my journey, if not long before.

30 August 1997

DAY 30

The Hotel

The great day has arrived. 'Yippee'. I hope they heard it all round the campsite. I am to pack the tent for the last time and move into a hotel. I had only seen the hotel from a distance. It looked presentable but not five star. Nevertheless, I had no qualms about moving from the campsite into what looked like a different civilisation. The room size was of no worry to me and I was unconcerned about that or what was provided for food at this stage. My dream was that it had a bed that was long enough for a six-footer, with a spring mattress and decent sheets. Sheets! I had almost forgotten what the word meant – little things mean a lot after a month on the road.

For once I could take my time packing the tent and loading the bike and not even care whether it looked tidy or not. As I packed, others were arriving and it was not long before the site was almost full. I guessed that the inevitable increased pressure on the amenities, even the clothes line, made this a good time to be moving on, and when I passed the campsite later in the week I could see that I had been right. Campers, mostly young, were arriving from early morning, mostly by car and occasionally on foot. I did not see one on a bike. All were tidy, with their camping gear carefully packed and easily managed. Tents were going up in no time, small stoves quickly lit and kettles were boiling. I began to realise what it meant to camp in style and how far I had been from it. Nevertheless, I could not look back on my experiences without some pride and fond nostalgia, knowing that I had done it the hard way and that I had succeeded. The candle had kept me moving and would burn bright in my memory for years to come.

The hotel was in walking distance and I intended to walk, pushing the bike along the roadside. I expected to meet my two daughters and my grandson, whom I had left snuggled up in bed as I began my journey a month ago, at some time in the late afternoon or evening. They were coming by car as their holiday time was more limited than mine and were taking the easy way and driving down through the east of France. They had booked the hotel some months earlier, being well aware that accommodation would be in short supply over the week of the championships. As I did not expect them until later in the day it made sense for me to find a safe park for my bike and while away my time wandering through the village.

It was typical of lakeside villages with as many houses as possible built to overlook the lake and to enjoy the rising and setting sun. The few shops were decked in readiness for the championships, with tourist items hanging temptingly in front of them. The flags of most of the counties involved in the racing were hung from whatever space the shopkeepers could find. Those of Eastern Europe were well represented, but the most common were those of France, Italy, Switzerland and Germany. The Union Flag was also in evidence. The main street was criss-crossed with bunting and welcome signs in several different languages. It was difficult not to get carried away with the sense of expectation and the growing excitement.

The *boulangerie* was already full by the time I reached it but the croissants and bread were as fresh as ever. The jabber of different languages increased my feeling of having arrived and my anticipation of the championships. I bought what few supplies I needed for lunch and then headed back to the campsite, where I had parked my bike. On the way I met a group of English supporters whom I recognised and had no hesitation in accepting their invitation to join them on a caravan site for a sort of a brunch. The chatter was pleasant, and the laughter only disturbed by the

175

serious conversation of one or two who were already into the forecasting of medallists and non-medallists. Most were interested in my journey and some appeared to be impressed. Whatever their reaction, I enjoyed the opportunity to spend some time in pleasant company before deciding to leave and head back to the campsite. I knew the tent was packed and the bike ready and that the clock was bringing me ever nearer to the hotel.

I arrived at the hotel mid-afternoon. The receptionist looked at me in surprise, dressed as I was in my usual flamboyant riding kit, and even more so when I asked, in my usual perfect French, '*Où est la place pour ma bicyclette?*' It was clear that such a request was unusual from the flutter it caused and the agitated telephone conversation that followed. Eventually the problem was solved and the bike wheeled into an old shed at the rear of the establishment. I took what I thought I needed from the panniers and was then shown to my room. Wonderful! The bed was long and springy, the sheets soft and white as snow. A quick shower and then I was lounging on the quilt on top of the bed. It was just as I was relaxing into sleep when the door opened and the family, or half of it, walked in. Kisses and hugs followed along with a myriad of questions about my journey, how I felt and had I met anyone of repute either while travelling or since I had arrived? It is strange how such seemingly insignificant family occasions impact on the memory and live with one forever.

Gradually everyone settled down and began to think more positively about how we were going to sleep. I was aware that my room contained two single beds and it was no surprise when it was announced that my grandson would be sharing the room with me. He did not seem to mind and there was certainly no reason for me to as I had a soft bed to myself. The family unpacked and then decided it was time to go and look for food. They had been travelling all day, living off sandwiches I gathered, and now they were going to take advantage of what the village's eating establishments had to offer. Not surprisingly, we were a few of many looking for food and took some time to find somewhere suitable. Eventually, we settled and ate in rather cramped conditions in what looked like somebody's front room. There was no doubt that the locals were keen to make the most of the championships!

31 August 1997

DAY 31

The first morning after sleeping in a bed for a month! The night had been wonderful, made the more so by sharing the room with my grandson, with the mattress shaping to my body in a way that the floor of a tent will never do. To stretch and not feel feet protruding through the tent door and to turn without disturbing the paraphernalia which usually surrounded my sleeping bag was a joy.

Even so, I rose early, as I had throughout my journey, and wandered downstairs in search of the fresh morning air. It was as I was relaxing at the door of the hotel that the Great Britain four (Foster, Pinsent, Redgrave and Cracknell) came by at what could only be described as a steady jog. I knew them well and so it was no surprise when they stopped to have a rest and a chat while supposedly having a warm-up run at the express command of their coach, who was not to be disobeyed, that was when they were within his sight. Their approach reminded me to some extent of the days at school when the class, during physical education, was sent on cross-country runs. Inevitably, half the class managed to find somewhere to stop for a smoke, usually under a railway bridge out of sight of the master's binoculars, while the keen ones among us tried to get round the three and a half miles.

This morning was different, however. They had staggering news to share. Princess Diana had been killed in a motor accident! They were clearly upset and disturbed by the news and wanted to talk to somebody about it and I happened to be available. Nobody knew the exact circumstances but the news bulletins were full of it. There was no mistake. The shock was great for the five of us, as it was to be for all of the British team and supporters as the news spread. Questions were being asked as I wandered towards the rowing course. Was the team going to be forbidden to race in the championships out of respect? Was the whole team to be called back to Britain? What should the race organisers do? I was struck by the way the tragedy affected not only the British, but many others from different countries. A cloud seemed to descend on what was normally an occasion of exciting challenge. How were the questions to be resolved?

For me, the tragedy was to become a reminder of the main purpose of my journey. I had come to light my own candle, an act which was now enabling me to gather strength from the past to live in the future. Little was I to know that a nation was now to light thousands of candles with much the same sentiments for the most gracious of princesses.

Late in the afternoon I sat outside and reflected on the days and nights passed, the affinity that had developed between myself, my bike, the tent and the rain. There had been sunny days, probably more than I could remember, but my lasting impression was of the days I had been exercised with rain. I looked back upon my friends the ants and especially the *moustiques* and could still see some of the scars they had bestowed upon me. The beautiful places I had passed through, perhaps my favourite being Avignon, though Rocamadour was a close second, flashed through my mind. I hoped that I could properly recall the impact their different features had had upon me when recounting the tale of my journey to others. I was aware that I was a fitter man than the one who had left England, one who had improved flexibility in arms and legs, a sharper eye, and one who was capable of covering much greater distances by bicycle than had been thought possible at the outset. I was surprised at how adept I had become in developing systems to organise my pannier and sort out my daily change of clothes. I thought about the skills I had developed in order to cope with the journey, some simple, such as taking a drink while riding, some more difficult, such as pitching a tent in different types of weather, always seeking to make it comfortable for the night.

But above all, I reminisced about my previous life with my wife and family and the opportunity that the journey had given me to consider how the joys of the past were likely to help me face my life of the future. The candle had worked its magic! It had given me a purpose and an opportunity to thank Andrea, in a spiritual act, for all she had meant to me. I hoped that it would go some way to meeting what she had often said in the worst trials of her illness, 'I feel a great calm, someone must be praying for me', and which is now engraved on her tombstone. Whatever was to happen in the future, my memory of her would remain as bright as the lighted candle.